FROM WORD *to* WORSHIP

FROM WORD *to* WORSHIP

How the Lectionary Welcomes You into Sacred Time Through Story, Symbol, and Sacrament

MICHAEL NIEBAUER

BakerBooks
a division of Baker Publishing Group
Grand Rapids, Michigan

Published by Baker Books
a division of Baker Publishing Group
Grand Rapids, Michigan
BakerBooks.com

Printed in the United States of America

Library of Congress Cataloging-in-Publication Data
Names: Niebauer, Michael, author
Title: From word to worship : how the lectionary welcomes you into sacred time through story, symbol, and sacrament / Michael Niebauer.
Description: Grand Rapids, Michigan : Baker Books, a division of Baker Publishing Group, [2026] | Includes appendixes. | Includes bibliographical references. | Audience term: Clergy | Audience term: Christians
Identifiers: LCCN 2026008109 | ISBN 9781540906090 paperback | ISBN 9781493465392 ebook
Subjects: LCSH: Common lectionary (1992) | Lectionary preaching
Classification: LCC BV4235.L43 N54 2026
LC record available at https://lccn.loc.gov/2026008109

Cover design by Sarah Gordon

Baker Publishing Group publications use paper produced from sustainable forestry practices and postconsumer waste whenever possible.

26 27 28 29 30 31 32 7 6 5 4 3 2 1

For Gabriel Zion

Gracious God and most merciful Father, you have granted us the rich and precious jewel of your holy Word: Assist us with your Spirit, that the same Word may be written in our hearts to our everlasting comfort, to reform us, to renew us according to your own image, to build us up and edify us into the perfect dwelling place of your Christ, sanctifying and increasing in us all heavenly virtues; grant this, O heavenly Father, for Jesus Christ's sake. Amen.

Prayer for Inner Renewal Through the Word
(2019 Book of Common Prayer)

CONTENTS

INTRODUCTION

Scripture and Sacred Time

Devote yourself to the public reading of Scripture, to preaching and to teaching.

1 Tim. 4:13 NIV

These are my words that I spoke to you while I was still with you—that everything written about me in the law of Moses, the prophets and the psalms must be fulfilled.

Luke 24:44

For I do not want you to be ignorant of the fact, brothers and sisters, that our ancestors were all under the cloud and that they all passed through the sea. They were all baptized into Moses in the cloud and in the sea. They all ate the same spiritual food and drank the

> same spiritual drink; for they drank from the spiritual rock that accompanied them, and that rock was Christ.
>
> 1 Cor. 10:1–4 NIV

EACH SUNDAY for the first eighteen years of my life, I heard a set of four Bible readings read out loud at church: one from the Psalms, one from the rest of the Old Testament, one from the Gospels, and one from the rest of the New Testament. These readings were part of a three-year schedule of passages known as the lectionary. But after nearly a thousand continuous Sundays, I could not articulate any discernible connection between the passages that were read each week. Furthermore, these readings seemed completely disconnected from the rest of worship. I was not alone, as most people in the pews were similarly stupefied. Our pastor was unable to tease out the relationships between these readings and their connection to the rest of the service, choosing instead to preach from the Gospel text and quickly jumping to its moral implications for our lives. Instead of preaching that showed how four passages of Scripture could form our worship of God through Jesus Christ, we heard sermons that were centered on one reading of Scripture and preaching that mostly focused on being a good person and a good Christian.

I can't blame my pastor for his failure to preach from all the readings each week. The reincorporation of readings from the Old Testament Torah and Prophets had only occurred in the Roman Catholic Church with the launch of The Lectionary for Mass (LCM) in 1970, and a similar incorporation of these passages in Protestant churches followed with the adoption of the Common Lectionary in 1983 and the Revised Common Lectionary (RCL) in 1992. The impetus for these new lectionaries was a renewal of interest in the reading, thinking, and worship practices of the early church, which spread from Roman Catholic to Protestant academic circles throughout the mid-twentieth century. Part of this renewal included a discovery of the extensive use of the Old Testament within ancient church worship, and the vast differences between ancient and modern approaches to the Bible in general.

The LCM and the RCL were attempts to incorporate these discoveries into the life of the contemporary church through a massive revision to the lectionaries that were being used in Roman Catholic and mainline Protestant churches. The most prominent of these revisions was the formation of a three-year cycle of readings to replace a single-year cycle, and the inclusion of Old Testament readings each Sunday. These Old Testament selections (or *lections*) were largely chosen to relate in some way to the major themes present in the Gospel reading for that Sunday.

As a theological and institutional initiative, the creation of these new lectionaries was a smashing success. With their adoption, centuries-old habits of listening to passages were changed and expanded. As an example, if you were a lay Roman Catholic living in 1576, 1745, or 1956, you would have heard a passage from the Old Testament, other than the Psalms, read three times a year. Now, you would hear the Old Testament read out loud nearly every

Sunday. Furthermore, the incorporation of these lectionaries remains perhaps the most successful ecumenical initiative ever, with a large number of Protestant churches adopting an RCL that was nearly identical to the Roman Catholic LCM. On a typical Sunday today, a Lutheran farmer in Minnesota will hear an almost identical set of readings as a Catholic businessman in Poland.

But for all of these achievements, the desire to retrieve ancient scriptural reading practices, and with it a love of the Old Testament, was unrealized. My experience growing up in a Roman Catholic Church in the '80s and '90s is still typical in a majority of churches that use a lectionary today. Parishioners still have little understanding of the relationship between the lectionary readings and their place within the overall church calendar. Pastors largely ignore a majority of lectionary texts when preaching, focusing on either the Epistle or Gospel reading or developing some form of sermon series from a single book of the Bible.

The reasons for this lack of advancement are numerous. Roman Catholicism, particularly in the West, suffers from substantial biblical illiteracy. Dogmatic and moral theology dominate most Roman Catholic seminaries, and many clergy lack the familiarity with the entirety of the Christian canon necessary to preach from multiple texts at a time. Many mainline churches have abandoned orthodox understandings of the authority of Scripture and have developed an aversion to preaching from lections of the Bible now deemed to be offensive. Baptist, Pentecostal, and evangelical churches have largely refrained from using lectionaries altogether. Preaching in these churches often focuses on expositing a small selection from a single book of the Bible, or topical sermons with occasional biblical references. While some of these churches have sought to retrieve certain ancient church practices, from Good Friday services to more frequent communion to the recitation of creeds, few have sought to recover the lectionary as a guide for Sunday Scripture recitation.

Yet I believe there is so much unrealized potential in the lectionary. When churches read all four prescribed passages each Sunday of the three-year cycle, they are exposed to a majority of the New Testament and the Psalter, and a significant portion of the Old Testament. They get to see how the seasons of the church calendar orient Christian time around the life, death, resurrection, and ascension of Jesus Christ. They are able to see how God has woven together stories and writings over thousands of years into one beautiful tapestry, and how each and every passage of Scripture holds the possibility of a direct encounter with God the Father through his Son, Jesus Christ, when read in the power of the Holy Spirit.

Ancient Approaches to Scripture: Time, Christ, and Liturgy

The LCM and RCL were part of a larger attempt to recover ancient approaches to the Bible that were lost or forgotten in the eighteenth and nineteenth centuries. Beginning in the mid-twentieth century, a number of theologians sought to uncover what precisely was lost in the changes to biblical interpretation that occurred during these centuries. As a result of their research, it is now possible to understand the unique approach to Scripture of the early Christians, how lectionaries were a natural outgrowth of their understanding of Scripture, and how their approach differs from modern biblical exegetical practices. These early Christian understandings of Scripture can be characterized by their unique approach to *time*, *Christ*, and *liturgy*.

Time. Scripture is both time-bound and timeless. As the product of human authors written at specific times and places, it details a linear history of the world from beginning to end. However, it is also the Word and words of God, who is outside and above creation and so outside and above time: "With the Lord a day is like a thousand years, and a thousand years are like a day" (2 Pet. 3:8 NIV). An encounter with God through the words of Scripture thus invites hearers to transcend time even as they remain in time, experiencing past and future events as if they were present. In this way they encounter God in sacred time.

An analogy to the human experience is helpful here. When I meet with a friend, past and future help to inform my present, and the present in turn changes my assessment of past and future. Past conversations with my friend set the groundwork for what is discussed. The present encounter might cause me to reevaluate my perception of our past relationship. In tense moments, an image of a caring act in the past keeps me from becoming quarrelsome. In a serene moment of our exchange, a vision of the two of us in retirement is formed, giving me hope that our friendship will endure for decades.

An encounter with God in Scripture is like this kind of personal encounter. God converses with us through his Word in the present. In this encounter, the words, exhortations, symbols, and events of Scripture, both past and future, rush into the present. One hears a passage about forgiveness and receives a picture of the cross. Another passage speaks of judgment, and a vision from Revelation rushes into the mind. Little bits of Scripture—sentences, symbols, persons, and events—can come together in a present intimate encounter with the God who is above time. Events from the past can inform the present and vice versa, and God can use specific parts of Scripture to refer to multiple things in multiple times and places. Each individual scriptural text can refer "to a range of entities, time-bound or not, and often at once; and Scripture's language serves to open up ourselves to this multivalent reality."[1]

Scripture is the Word of God and the accounts of God's wondrous works within the world. Early Christians assumed that God had orchestrated and arranged the entirety of Scripture so that all of it—little bits and large sections, persons, actions, and symbols—could be brought to bear on the present experiences of his church. Approaching Scripture within this heavenly context of sacred time naturally lent itself to reading selections from various books of the Bible together. The reading out loud of these lections together invited the hearer to see how their accounts of past and future could be made present before them as they sat in sacred time. Such an approach to Scripture was already at work within the Old Testament tabernacle, temple, and synagogue gatherings. As Israel read the Torah within these sacred gatherings, they were compelled to stack lections from the Prophets and Writings that related to the Torah passage, in a process known as *haruzin* (pearl stringing).[2] Jewish sermons likewise flowed out of this process, with the preacher adding additional passages and examples that were linked in some way to the Torah selection.

This process, however, was limited in what it could accomplish, since the Israelite temple was "only a copy" and not the true heavenly temple. Christ needed to ascend in order to open up the heavenly temple and allow us into sacred time, and it is in Christ alone that these Old Testament selections find their true fulfillment. Israelite *haruzin* played the third and fifth of the chord, yearning for the resolve that would come in the root of Jesse.

Christ. The Israelites were limited in their ability to encounter the living God and thus limited in the ways in which they could bring all of Scripture to bear on their encounters with him. But with the advent of Jesus Christ, the people of God are now afforded the opportunity to personally encounter the author of all of Scripture. Jesus is the Word of God, the fulfillment of the entirety of Scripture. We see this most vividly at the beginning of Jesus's earthly ministry. While in synagogue, he is granted the opportunity to read from the scroll of Isaiah, which was most likely read in conjunction with a lection from the Torah. When Jesus stands up to *haruzin*, string together these passages, he declares that the readings are fulfilled in him (Luke 4:21). Later, before he ascends to the Father,

Jesus declares to his followers, "These are my words that I spoke to you while I was still with you—that everything written about me in the law of Moses, the prophets, and the psalms must be fulfilled" (24:44).

In the wake of Pentecost, Jesus's disciples preached of the resurrection and explained how all of the Old Testament is now fulfilled in Jesus. The churches that they founded continued to unpack the mystery of Christ as revealed in every single jot and tittle of the Old Testament. As it expanded, the early church continued the synagogue process of reading out loud lections from the Old Testament, increasingly incorporating into these readings passages from newly written Gospels and apostolic writings. Christ remained the focal point of these compilations, which eventually became formalized through the development of *lection*-aries. Because Christ is the center of Scripture, these lectionaries made the Gospels their focal point, replacing the centrality of the Torah. The schedule for these readings in turn followed the Gospels through the life, death, resurrection, ascension, and second coming of Jesus Christ, which were codified in the seasons of Advent, Christmas, Epiphany, Lent, and Easter.

Liturgy. Early Christian interpreters assumed a timeless quality to Scripture: its ability to draw together past, present, and future in an immediate encounter with God. They also asserted Christ as the fulfillment of all of Scripture and the key to understanding its contents. The resurrected Christ unlocks the true meaning of the Old Testament, allowing it to speak of him and be applied directly and immediately to those who read it in him. These first two approaches to Scripture in turn had profound ramifications on how Christians understood their communal life, since the Old Testament contains detailed commands and descriptions concerning the ways in which the people of God are called to assemble for worship.

The Old Testament introduces a number of symbols, words, and actions that are meant to structure common worship, beginning in the tabernacle and later in the temple. Christ fulfills these passages of Scripture by reorienting the entire worship and sacrificial system to himself, seen most vividly in the reorientation of the Passover meal to his death. We see in the Last Supper a taking up of Old Testament symbol and action into the life of Christ for the sake of his followers. The early Christians simply carried on this process, plumbing the depths of Scripture to see how the entirety of its symbols point to Christ: Water is baptism, tree is cross, and fire is Spirit. The liturgies that developed drew directly on these Old Testament symbols, and biblical interpretation sought to deepen the experience of liturgical worship through these symbols.

But the point of such endeavors was not novelty or the search for happy coincidences. Since the Old Testament is living history for the church, its symbols and events are able to add to our understanding of Christ and the Christian life. So the crossing of the Red Sea is not just a story that *resembles* Christian baptism; it is a story *about* Christian baptism (1 Cor. 10:2), and from it Christians may grow in their understanding of baptism. Likewise, the sacrifices in Leviticus are about the sacrifice of Christ as it is experienced in the Eucharist. The process of discovering these connections between Old Testament, New Testament, and liturgy was ongoing, a ceaseless mining of the infinite riches of Scripture.

As the new tabernacling people of God, the church assembly afforded a unique opportunity to enter sacred time, creating a symbolically charged environment that encouraged preachers to draw out more and more of these connections. Breaking bread each Sunday invited the hearers of Scripture to connect this act with the bestowal of heavenly manna. The lighting of candles naturally called to mind the fire of the Holy Spirit and the fire of judgment. Worshipers were invited to experience these events in sacred time, and the lectionaries that were compiled out of these church gatherings in turn reflected this symbolic reality. Lections from various parts of the Bible connected Old Testament, New Testament, and Christian worship.

Demise of the Lectionary

The use of lectionaries was the product of a specific ancient way of approaching Scripture, one that asserted the ability of various passages to speak both multidirectionally and simultaneously, one that affirmed the centrality of Christ as the one who draws together these passages, and one that leveraged the entirety of Scripture to inform and nourish the church's worship. As a result, the reception of Scripture in the form of lections organized around the church calendar was the principal way that most Christians encountered God's Word for centuries. However, aspects of this approach to Scripture diminished over time.

The first signs of this diminishment could be seen as far back as the Middle Ages, with the removal of most of the Old Testament from Roman Catholic Sunday lectionaries.

But the biggest changes in understandings of Scripture, changes that made the lectionary superfluous at best, began as a product of various intellectual movements known collectively as the Enlightenment. In Enlightenment Europe, the locus of proper interpretation slowly moved from the church to the academy, with the goal being first and foremost an accurate reconstruction of the original historical and literary context of individual passages of Scripture. It was the job of scholars to reconstruct this original context, with spiritual and moral instruction occurring *after* this initial step was completed and deemed satisfactory by academic standards.

Such an approach to Scripture emphasized the secular, linear, and historical aspects of Scripture to the detriment of its sacred, eternal, and participatory aspects. While many scholars who used the so-called historical-critical method abandoned core tenets of Christian orthodoxy, this approach became dominant even for those who maintained orthodoxy and remains the principal approach for many today. For example, a popular textbook by Scott Duvall and Daniel Hays asserts that biblical interpretation should begin with a reconstruction of the "original" context of a specific passage of Scripture, using historical, literary, and lexical aides as needed. After this process, one then crosses "the principlizing bridge," seeking to apply the scriptural text to contemporary moral and spiritual life.[3] Likewise, Gordon Fee and Douglas Stuart assert that "a text cannot mean what it never could have meant to its author or readers."[4] The critical realism of N. T. Wright similarly emphasizes the necessity of historical reconstruction and de-emphasizes the ability of Scripture to produce multiple meanings.[5]

There are benefits to be gleaned from this approach. Scripture comes to us through historically bound writings, and it chronicles real events that occurred in secular history. Modern historical criticism aided the church in better understanding these historical and linear aspects of Scripture, and in turn has helped Christians understand the contours of salvation history. However, in cutting off the spiritual, timeless understandings of Scripture, this approach has severed the connections between time, Christ, and worship that were hallmarks of early Christian interpretation, and from which the production of lectionaries was a natural outflow. First, the reduction of Scripture to an artifact principally of secular time limited Scripture's ability to speak multidirectionally. In this approach, "out of context," meaning "out of historical context as discerned by current scholarly consensus," was code for misinterpretation. Hence the crossing of the Red Sea could no longer be a passage about Christian baptism, as it was for the early Christians. The sacrifice of Isaac could no longer be about the resurrection of Christ, as it was for the author of Hebrews. Such interpretations cannot pass the historical-critical scholar's test of meaning, since they were clearly not how these texts were understood by their original audiences.

A focus almost exclusively on the linear, historical aspects of Scripture naturally led to a diminishment of lectionaries, since lectionaries intentionally ripped selections of Scripture *out of context* without requiring historical reconstruction. In its place emerged expository preaching, which focuses on one biblical book, leveraging academic commentaries in order to help reconstruct the original context of the chosen text. Later, topical sermons arose in which an issue pertinent to the congregation is discerned by the pastor, who then constructs a sermon that pulls in biblical verses that speak to the issue at hand.

With the decline of the lectionary and of Scripture's ability to be read in sacred time, the Christocentric nature of all of Scripture was lost and forgotten. This is a natural result of an interpretation of Scripture that limits the meaning of any section to one historical referent. Here, the Bible becomes *only* a story of creation, fall, and redemption, with discrete, punctiliar events that progress along a linear timeline. The Old Testament, since it was written before the coming of Christ, lost its ability to speak directly about Christ. The Old Testament could point forward to Christ (as is the case with the Prophets) but could not speak directly to a present encounter with Christ.

Since the Old Testament could only point forward to Christ, it was rendered functionally superfluous.[6] It became a kind of prequel history, interesting to die-hard fans of Scripture but never as important as the New Testament readings that speak directly about Christ. At its worst, this approach to Scripture rendered large portions of the Old

Testament problematic. Passages concerning military conquest, which were used by the early church to explain the necessity of slaying the passions for the development of Christian virtue, could no longer carry this kind of meaning in any real sense. Instead, these passages became only disturbing accounts of unjustified warfare whose singular meaning must be delicately navigated by the preacher (or, more likely, never discussed in public). The superfluous or problematic nature of much of the Old Testament led to its diminishment in church assemblies. Today, even many churches that still use the lectionary avoid the Old Testament as a regular part of their preaching.

The reduction of Scripture to a singular historically reconstructed meaning in turn diminished the capacity of the Bible to speak directly to the experience of Christ in the worship and sacramental life of the church. Levitical sacrifices, by definition, cannot be about the Eucharist in any real or direct way. Interpreters of Scripture were explicitly encouraged to *not* try to make such connections between Old Testament, New Testament, and liturgy. To do so would bring about accusations of eisegesis.

It is not coincidental that the rise of the historical-critical method was concurrent with the rise of church assemblies that were devoid of symbol and sacrament. The Old Testament is where the symbols and actions of Christian worship are introduced, and these texts are meant to nourish the church's continual doxological life. But these texts are now effectively dead, leaving only a small amount of material in the New Testament that directly addresses the church's common life of worship. Even in churches that retained the historic shape of the liturgy, there remains a kind of symbolic rupture between the two parts of the church service. The reading of Scripture and eucharistic celebration appear as two discrete and unrelated events. Preaching focuses mostly on expounding the Gospel passage, rarely touching on the Old Testament lectionary readings or showing how Scripture integrally relates to the various aspects of worship.

About This Book

The goal of this book is to help unlock the potential of the lectionary to disciple Christians to approach Scripture along the same vector as the early church. On a basic level, I hope that a Christian attending a church that uses the RCL, LCM, BCP or similar lectionaries will have a better grasp of the key themes of the church year and a better understanding of how those themes are manifested in the Old Testament and New Testament selections. To aid in this task, I will focus particularly on key symbols that emerge within these readings. Symbols such as trees, fire, wind, and water serve as binding agents in Scripture, tying together various biblical passages to the life, death, and resurrection of Christ. The lectionary frequently draws out these connections, both within specific Sundays and within specific seasons of the church year. These symbols are key to understanding how Scripture itself is knit together and how the lectionary can help to immerse individuals in the world of Scripture through these symbols.

Scripture trains us to see the world through its words and its symbols. It is the key to seeing Christ's presence in the material world. As the lectionary trains us to see the interconnectedness of the stories and symbols of the Bible, it will open us up to the ways in which its stories and symbols are manifested in the physical actions of the church as it worships. This book in turn will tease out these connections between Old Testament, New Testament, and the liturgical practices of the church. As you begin to read Scripture in this way, you should begin to draw these connections together yourself. For instance, as you hear the word *bread* in the recitation of Scripture, you should instantly connect this word with manna in the desert, the bread multiplied by Jesus, and your experience of tasting the body of Christ at communion.

In my earlier book *Four Mountains*, I described this approach as an exploration of both the melody and harmony of Scripture. We can use the symbols and events of each book of the Bible to better understand its underlying chronological narrative, just as sequential notes on a music staff chart the melody of a song. In addition, we can take these same symbols and events and stack them together to deepen our understanding of Jesus Christ, just as one stacks musical notes together to make harmonious chords. We can then weave our own experiences into these stories and symbols, enriching our encounter with Christ. While *Four Mountains* uses this approach to chart the overall biblical story from Genesis to Revelation, this book focuses on the melody of the church calendar and the harmony of the lectionary passages. The "melody" of the book goes from Advent through Ordinary Time, while the "harmony" is shown in the ways that the lectionary readings for each Sunday are stitched together by common symbols and themes.

On the RCL and the Structure of This Book

This book covers the major themes and symbols throughout a majority of the RCL, though it does not include each and every week. Instead, I will focus on the "synchronous" passages of the lectionary, those that are intentionally collated together around common themes and symbols. There are, however, certain weeks that contain passages that are not interconnected. During Ordinary Time, the RCL has two "tracks" of readings. The Old Testament readings for track 1 are not correlated with the Gospel passage, so I will largely ignore these readings, instead drawing from the track 2 Old Testament passages. The Epistle readings for portions of the church year are often uncorrelated to the Gospel passage, and so will likewise be ignored. The purpose of the incorporation of these "continuous" readings was to help parishioners encounter larger swaths of Scripture in public worship. However, I find their incorporation to be unnecessary. Ordinary Time is already a season that gives pastors flexibility to modify lectionary readings, so if pastors would like to do a deep dive on a specific book of the Bible, they should be free to make whatever adjustments needed. Those who desire a lengthy discussion on one specific book of the Bible should likewise seek out one of the legions of commentaries already in existence. Nevertheless, since the possible connections between the various books of Scripture are endless, individuals will eventually learn to see connections even in these linear selections. Appendix A features my own modification of the lectionary, which removes these continuous selections in favor of lections that are integrally related to the Gospel passages each week.

Since the RCL contains a similar structure to the LCM, the Book of Common Prayer (BCP) lectionary, and other lectionaries, it should be a helpful guide for anyone who encounters Scripture through a lectionary of some kind. In order to help cover the range of churches that use a lectionary, I have begun each chapter with a prayer drawn from various prayer books.

CHAPTER 1

JUDGMENT

Christ Brings Fire

All Years: Proper 27, 28, 29, Advent 1, 2, 3

O God, whose blessed Son came into the world that he might destroy the works of the devil and make us children of God and heirs of eternal life: Grant that, having this hope, we may purify ourselves as he is pure; that, when he comes again with power and great glory, we may be made like him in his eternal and glorious kingdom; where he lives and reigns with you and the Holy Spirit, one God, for ever and ever. Amen.

Collect for Proper 27 (2019 BCP)

EACH LECTIONARY YEAR ends and begins with a series of readings that center upon the second coming of Jesus, with the last three weeks of each year bleeding into the first weeks of Advent for the ensuing year. The readings and prayers for these weeks, which are called *propers*, serve as a bridge between Ordinary Time and Advent, as the Gospel readings slowly move from discussions about the second coming of Jesus to the events preceding his first coming at Bethlehem.

The principal theme of these Sunday readings is judgment. Christians declare in the creeds that Christ "will come again to judge the living and the dead," and the Old Testament, Epistle, and Gospel readings serve to unpack a Christian understanding of judgment especially as it pertains to Christ's second coming. The Old Testament selections draw extensively from the Prophets, whose invocations of divine judgment are meant to be read in the present and future tense: God's judgment on the iniquities of Israel is the very same judgment on unrepentant sin in the church today, and God's final judgment provides the same comfort for the persecuted church as it did for the embattled Israel of the prophets. The Gospel readings are paired with these prophetic selections and likewise serve as a present warning and future comfort for Christians today. In order to tease out the practical implications of Christ's judgment for the local congregation, these lectionary readings draw extensively on Paul's letters to the Thessalonians, as these epistles are simultaneously apocalyptic and pastoral.

Four symbols help to stitch together these lectionary passages. Each symbol is manifested in both the Old Testament and New Testament, and viewed together, they paint a robust picture of the scope of Christ's judgment and its implications for the church today. First, the symbol of *darkness* describes the present state of the world as one still in need of final judgment. Then, the symbols of *separation* and *fire* are used to describe the ways that Christ will execute his final judgment on the world. Finally, in view of the reality of this present darkness and the impending separation of the world, the figure of *watchfulness* is deployed in order to exhort the church to prepare for this final judgment.

In this chapter, I will unpack the theme of judgment through an examination of each of these four symbols as they occur in the lectionary readings. Then I will show how the church experiences the judgment of Christ through contemporary practices such as the lighting of candles, the enactment of membership requirements, and the excommunication of the unrepentant.

Darkness

When we wake up in the middle of the night, we are disoriented and fearful. Unaware of our surroundings, we stumble and fall. The random noises that we ignore in the light now haunt us, and we wonder if they are portents of some calamity or intrusion. This fear of the night was heightened in the days before electricity, when darkness could not be alleviated with the flick of a switch. But we are still reminded of the perils of darkness whenever we are caught alone on a moonless night on a city street or in a dense forest. Darkness is a sign of evil, chaos, and disorder.

The propers preceding Advent depict the period preceding Christ's return as one marked by "darkness and gloom" (Zeph. 1:15). Proper 28A weaves the symbol of darkness throughout the entirety of its readings, with Paul reminding the Thessalonians that the last day will come like a thief in the night (1 Thess. 5:1–11) and Jesus's parable of the talents ending with the worthless slave being cast into the darkness (Matt. 25:30). The readings from the end of Ordinary Time and the beginning of Advent expand on the content of this darkness: Jesus states that thc approaching last judgment will be marked by wars, famine (Mark 13:7–8, 28B; Luke 21:9–11, 28C), and chaos and disorder (Mark 13:24–25, Advent 1B).

These readings make it clear that the time leading up to the last day—the entire history between the birth of Christ and his second coming—is marked not by the gradual improvement of humankind but by a never-ending cycle of sin, chaos, and destruction. Augustine teases out this point when recounting the entirety of known history in *The City of God*: There has never been a truly just civilization, since none have Jesus Christ as their center.[1] As the light of Christ, the church is the one and only community that will endure through this darkness. Yet even the church is not immune to the destructive elements of sin.

The day of the Lord has not yet arrived, and an emphasis on this present darkness is meant to caution Christians against a false optimism. When people become Christians, they do receive the light of Christ and can experience the fruit of the Spirit internally through a changed heart. They also get a glimpse of this light shining through in their physical experience with others in the church. However, this light is still a small flicker in a sea of darkness, and we should never presume that sin has been fully eradicated from the individual, the church, or the community.

Those who ignore the reality of an ever-present darkness, who set their hopes on human machinations, are doomed to cycles of optimism followed by inevitable despair. They become convinced that the world will be fixed if only the right civil programs are enacted and the right politicians elected. However, they soon discover that very little changes even when cultural and political victories are won.

Similarly, Christians can fall into despair over the state of the church if they fail to acknowledge the reality of this present darkness. While the church is a pilgrim community that will last until the second coming of Christ, individual churches are themselves a mixture of light and darkness, of sinners and saints. Just as sin is a diminishing yet still present part of the Christian soul, sin is still an ever-present reality in the life of the church. Those who demand perfection from their local church will fall into a similar cycle of optimism and despair—hopping from one church to another, initially enthused by surface perfections, but ultimately leaving in disillusionment once the underlying warts are exposed. Paul's second letter to the Thessalonians (3:6–13, 28C) helps Christians protect against this false optimism by highlighting the mundane realities of life in the church: Even the early Christian communities had to deal with lazy freeloaders in their midst!

The biblical description of present darkness is meant to lift Christians out of these cycles of optimism and despair by inviting them to set their hopes on the future return of the Lord. While there is healing and holiness in the church, it is still a community in need of further healing, yearning for a future perfection that will come through the returning Christ. And while there are moments where the actions of the church make a real and profound impact on the world, Christians know that whatever social, political, or cultural gains are made are only temporary. They are relieved of the burden of having to "change the world," and are free to proclaim the gospel, heal the sick, and care for the poor, not expecting that their efforts will usher in a permanent utopia.

Separation

The lectionary readings speak to the reality of darkness in a world still tainted by sin. While Christians have access to the light of Christ from the moment of their conversion, they know that this light flickers in a still-dark world. They long for the day when this darkness will be separated from the light, when evil works and evil people will be banished from the world.

An act of judgment is an act of separation. The purpose of judgment is to clearly delineate good from bad, better from worse, and right from wrong. A trial, for instance, takes the murky facts of a crime and distills them into a clear, definitive, and final judgment on the accused: guilty or innocent. Those who long for justice long for good judgment, for someone to acknowledge the harm done to them and separate the offenders through a declaration of guilt, thus creating space for the innocent to live in peace. But human judgment is imperfect and weak. We live in a world where the guilty frequently go unpunished, the innocent are condemned, and systemic injustices are impossible to overcome. The present experiences of flawed judgment stir in the heart of the Christian a longing for a complete and perfect judgment, where evil will be completely separated from good.

The lectionary readings thus describe the final judgment of Christ as an act of separation. Ezekiel 34:11–17 (29A) vividly portrays this separation as a great rescue and sorting. God the Good Shepherd judges between sheep, rescuing his own sheep out of darkness and banishing those opposed to him. This is echoed in the Jeremiah readings for 29C (23:1–6) and Advent 1C (33:14–16). Jesus describes a sudden separation, where "two will be in the field; one will be taken, and one will be left" (Matt. 24:40, Advent 1A). The Gospel reading from 29C gives the most vivid example of the separation that will occur, and the need for all to acknowledge Christ as the final judge. Two thieves stand in agony on crosses that bracket the crucified Christ. One thief mocks Jesus, while the other acknowledges his kingship. The one who recognizes Jesus as true king and true judge is promised entrance into the heavenly kingdom (Luke 23:33–43). While both criminals are guilty, only the one that acknowledges Jesus as king is rescued from eternal judgment. His rescue comes not through some heroic deed of virtue, but by the acknowledgment of Jesus as the one true judge.

Fire

To those who acknowledge Jesus as true king and perfect judge, this separation will be experienced as a rescue from darkness. The assurance of this rescue is a present comfort to those Christians who are enduring injustice, hardship, and persecution. But to those who reject Jesus, this separation will be experienced as fire: "See, the day is coming, burning like an oven, when all the arrogant and all evildoers will be stubble; the day that comes shall burn them up, says the LORD of hosts, so that it will leave them neither root nor branch" (Mal. 4:1, 28C; see also Isa. 64:1–9, Advent 1B).

Fire swiftly consumes and destroys, turning complex organisms into simple dust and ash. Fire also performs a separating function in precious metals, removing dirt and impurities. A gold nugget, for instance, is refined in fire—the dirt eradicated in smoke, leaving the gleam of pure gold. The second coming of Jesus is portrayed as fire to highlight the swiftness and completeness of his judgment. Jesus will refine the entire world, separating and eradicating from it all sin, evil, and darkness. No molecule of creation can withstand the penetrating judgment of Christ. The declaration of a swift and fiery future judgment is meant to quicken the hearts of individuals in the present. Like the two thieves bracketing Jesus, we all stand as guilty sinners, and like them, we are all slated to die in our sin. We are all given the choice to reject Jesus or to ask Jesus to rescue us from this impending judgment. For those who accept Jesus, this image of a fiery future is meant to remind them of the seriousness with which they are called to grow in the love of God in the present. This present pursuit in the face of future judgment is described in Scripture as watchfulness.

Watchfulness

The final judgment of Christ will be marked by separation and fire, but the precise date of his second coming is unknown. As the lectionary moves from the close of Ordinary Time into the beginning of Advent, the readings focus more on the ways that Christians ought to behave in light of the revelation of a coming judgment. Jesus declares that only the Father knows the day and hour of judgment, and because of this uncertainty, Christians are called to be watchful: "Keep awake therefore, for you do not know on what day your Lord is coming. . . . Therefore you also must be ready, for the Son of Man is coming at an hour you do not expect" (Matt. 24:42, 44, Advent 1A). A similar exhortation is given in Advent 1B's Gospel reading: "Therefore, keep awake—for you do not know when the master of the house will come, in the evening or at midnight or at cockcrow or at dawn, or else he may find you asleep when he comes suddenly" (Mark 13:35–36).

Watchfulness is directly correlated with preparedness. Whenever we are watching for the arrival of an important guest, we prepare by meticulously cleaning our house, ensuring that everything from floor to ceiling is immaculate. Similarly, watching for the return of Christ prompts the Christian to do a kind of housecleaning of the soul: We examine every inch of our lives in order to discern whether each thought, word, and deed is being done for the glory of God or for the glory of the self. For John the Baptist, preparing the way of the Lord leads to repentance and reformation (Mark 1:1–8, Advent 2B; Luke 3:7–18, Advent 3C). For Peter, preparedness spurs active lives of holiness and good works: "Since all these things are to be dissolved in this way, what sort of persons ought you to be in leading lives of holiness and godliness, waiting for and hastening the coming of the day of God" (2 Pet. 3:11–12, Advent 2B).

The ill-prepared are those who focus only on worldly, temporal goods. They float through life seeking only comfort, pleasure, and success, rarely stopping to ask whether their actions have any meaning beyond their inevitable death. Such persons are fixated on the things that "are to be dissolved." The watchful, in contrast, are constantly finding new and creative ways to delight in and glorify God with their actions, knowing that the truth, goodness, and beauty ushered in by their actions bear the mark of eternity.

Experiencing Judgment in the Church Today

The lectionary readings provide a stock of symbols that enrich our understanding of judgment and the second coming of Jesus Christ. In both Sunday worship and its ongoing communal life, the church is afforded opportunities to experience Christ's judgment and anticipate his second coming. First, the antinomies of darkness and light are experienced as one enters the church sanctuary.

Before worship begins, the church is dark and the mood is somber as the congregation waits on the coming of Jesus in worship. Then candles are lit, light in the darkness, as a sign that the congregation is being given a temporary reprieve from the darkness of the world. The transition from darkness to light is starkest on Easter Vigil. Here, the service begins with the lighting of the Paschal Candle, and from there, the light passes to candles held by the rest of the congregation, with all singing "the darkness has been vanquished by our eternal king."[2] The extinguishing of these candles at the end of worship is a reminder that the church must descend back into the darkness of the world, toiling amid pain and brokenness until Jesus returns to bring the glory of the Lord to every inch of the earth.

While the illumination of a candle reminds the church of the brightness of Jesus, its flame reminds Christians of the fiery judgment that will come with his return. And though the candle reminds us of the light of Christ in the church, it is also meant to remind us of Christ's judgment on our souls. It prompts a searching of the soul for areas in need of refinement by the fire of the Holy Spirit. For Ignatius of Loyola, contemplation of fire was an immersive experience, encompassing the whole of the spiritual senses, as individuals are invited to imagine the fires of hell in their mind's eye, smelling its smoke and feeling the heat of its flames.[3] This awakens in the soul the seriousness of Christ's judgment on sinners and God's immense mercy on those who repent and believe.

When internalized in the spiritual senses, the fire of the candle sparks a period of self-reflection followed by repentance. Confession is perhaps the most important way that Christians stay watchful and alert, for confession requires an acceptance of Christ's judgment on human sin. In repentance, the words of John the Baptist and Isaiah intertwine with the voice of Christ in our soul, all exhorting us to prepare for the certain yet unexpected return of the true and perfect judge.

The church experiences and anticipates the separation that will come at the last judgment through the various ways it demarcates its committed members. Throughout large portions of Christian history, churches would dismiss visitors and catechumens after the reading of the Gospel, ceremonially shutting the doors of the church in order to bar them from the celebration of communion. Maximus the Confessor viewed this dismissal and the closing of the doors as a prefiguring of the second coming, where Jesus "will separate by the holy angels the faithful from the faithless."[4] This separation was meant to spur those interested in Christianity to continue on the path to baptism, warning them of the eternal separation that will occur if they reject Christ.

While fewer churches practice such sharp separations during corporate worship today, churches still practice separation through confirmation and membership classes. Here, the church draws distinctions between those who are committed to the ongoing life of the church and those who are not ready to commit. Such commitments bring with them certain privileges, such as the right to lead specific ministries or the right to have a voice in pressing matters of the congregation.

But perhaps the most visible sign of separation and judgment performed by the church comes through the act of excommunication. When one of its members has engaged in grievous sin that threatens the social fabric of the church, and when that member remains unrepentant, the church engages in a temporal act of judgment, casting that member out of the church and barring them from participation in the Eucharist. In such judgment, the unrepentant are cast out into the darkness, unto Satan for the destruction of their flesh (1 Cor. 5:5). However, such an act of judgment, which is granted by Jesus to the church, is not the final judgment upon the sinner. Instead, such expulsion is meant to inculcate in the unrepentant an awareness of the eternal judgment of Christ that awaits them, so that they might repent and be reconciled back into the life of the church. Excommunication of an individual is thus done with the hope that their "spirit might be saved in the day of the Lord" (v. 5).

Each year of the lectionary ends with an affirmation of a present darkness in the world, and each lectionary year begins with an exhortation to be watchful as we await the second coming of Jesus, when he will rescue the church out of darkness and into the eternal light and life of God. While Jesus will bring a fiery judgment upon the works of darkness in the world, he is also the revelation to the world of the light and glory of God. Judgment is meant to foster in Christians a deep yearning for this light to be revealed, and for God's glory to extend to all the ends of the earth.

As the lectionary moves from the end of Ordinary Time through the season of Advent, it moves the church from a focus on darkness and judgment to a focus on revelation and light. The Advent readings transition from an emphasis on the second coming to a focus on the coming light in the birth of Jesus Christ at Christmas, and the season of Epiphany will unpack the substance of this revelation. The next chapter picks up this theme of revelation through the symbol of light.

CHAPTER 2

GLORY

Christ Our Light

Advent 3A, Christmas I, III, Epiphany Day

O God, you have caused this holy night to shine with the brightness of the true Light: Grant that we, who have known the mystery of that Light on earth, may also enjoy him perfectly in heaven; where with you and the Holy Spirit he lives and reigns, one God, in glory everlasting. Amen.

Preface to Christmas (2019 BCP)

ADVENT IS THE SEASON in which the church acknowledges the darkness of a world still steeped in sin, which stirs a desire for this darkness to be scattered by the light of Christ. And so Advent gives way to Christmas and Epiphany, which celebrate the birth of Jesus Christ as the light of the world. These seasons focus specifically on Jesus Christ as the revelation of God's glory to the world. The lectionary texts in turn use the symbols of light, sun, and gold to deepen our understanding of God's glory and to help articulate the appropriate response of humanity to an encounter with God's glory.

Glory is used to describe occasions in which the inner beauty and goodness of a person or object is made visible to someone else. These moments of glorious revelation take place within the context of an intimate encounter between two persons or between a person and a work of art. For example, a Caravaggio painting can be viewed as little more than oil on canvas, a splash of pigment as mundane as an overturned paint can on a sidewalk. But when a dedicated observer sits and stares at this very same paint, an encounter can occur where the inner beauty of the masterpiece overwhelms the onlooker.

Such glorious encounters also take place on a person-to-person level. There are moments in friendship where the inner beauty of a friend is revealed, where the goodness and character of another person rise to the surface. We may even say in these moments that someone is "in their glory," or that they "have a glow about them." Couples sometimes describe the moment where they fall in love as this type of glorious encounter, where the inner beauty of their lover rises to the visible surface.

Human beings were created to delight in God's glory, to have the kind of intimate encounter with God in which God's inner beauty is revealed. In Eden, Adam and Eve were able to encounter some of God's inner beauty during their serene walks in the garden. But after they sinned, they were cast away from God's presence and glory. A personal, intimate encounter with God was now off-limits. The rest of the Pentateuch is the story of how God creates a way for humanity to encounter his glory once again, though the persistence of sin means that full access is still not possible.

But the prophecies of Advent are meant to stir a hope that one day all "shall see the glory of the LORD, the majesty of our God" (Isa. 35:2, Advent 3A). These Advent hopes are fulfilled in Christmas with the birth of Jesus Christ. The incarnation of Christ is both a manifestation of God's glory and the beginning of Jesus Christ's mission to enable human beings to access this glory. The lectionary readings for Christmas and Epiphany unpack the significance of this revelation of glory in Christ through the symbols of light and sun.

Light

The preeminent symbol of God's glory is light. Light illuminates and reveals what is hidden by darkness. This illuminative power of light is thus related to both knowledge and beauty. Light grants us knowledge of our material surroundings, allowing us to safely navigate the world around us. Light also enables us to see beautiful objects. This is why lighting is an integral part of so many art forms, from ballet to theater to the staging of museums. Proper lighting grants the observer a better opportunity to experience the beauty in these artifacts.

The lectionary readings for Christmas are meant to show the direct connection between light, glory, and the birth of Jesus. The opening salvo of Christmas I begins with Isaiah explicitly foretelling this connection: "The people who walked in darkness have seen a great light; those who lived in a land of deep darkness—on them light has shined. . . . For a child has been born for us, a son given to us; authority rests upon his shoulders; and he is named Wonderful Counselor, Mighty God, Everlasting Father, Prince of Peace" (Isa. 9:2, 6). The Gospel reading for Christmas I connects this passage with the birth of Jesus (Luke 2:1–14), and the reading from Titus explains that Jesus's birth is the "manifestation of the glory of our great God" (Titus 2:13).

The coming of Jesus as the coming of light and glory is most explicitly seen in the Christmas III readings, so important that they are to be used on a Sunday after Christmas if not used on Christmas Day. While the Hebrews reading for this Sunday declares that Jesus is the reflection of God's glory and the exact imprint of God's being (Heb. 1:1–4), the John passage draws together the titles of Word, life, and light to Jesus, culminating with the declaration that, in the incarnation, "the Word became flesh and dwelt among us, and we have seen his glory, glory as of the only Son from the Father, full of grace and truth" (John 1:14 ESV).

These passages make clear that the glory of God takes on flesh in Jesus Christ. The inner beauty of God is made manifest, made visible, in the flesh of Jesus Christ. As the light of the world, Jesus makes accessible the knowledge and beauty of God. But while this light is given to the whole world, the lectionary readings remind us that it is only the righteous who will have eyes to behold this glory (Ps. 97:11, Christmas II). Just as the beauty of a painting is only revealed to those who are willing to behold it, so the light of God's glory is only made known to those with inner eyes to see.

Sun and Star

A corollary symbol to light is the sun. As the celestial body that provides light to the entire earth, the sun is an appropriate symbol for the glory of God and helps to expand and enrich our understanding of God's glory in a number of ways. First, the light of the sun is inexhaustible. The light of the sun warms the planet, provides nutrients to plants, comforts human beings, and can even be harnessed by solar panels to provide electricity. Yet the sun's energy is not depleted by any of these objects or processes. Similarly, the light of the sun is ubiquitous—it is accessible at the same time by different people living thousands of miles apart. The light of the sun does not discriminate in the light that it sheds. A mother in Argentina grasps the same light as a child in Alberta.

The light of the sun is also a source of comfort and joy. There is a certain indefinable joy that overtakes a human on the first sunny day after a week of clouds and rain. The absence of the sun can have a deleterious physiological impact on many human beings who suffer each year from seasonal affective disorder. Finally, our sense of time is oriented around the sun. Days are marked by the rising and falling of the sun. Years are marked by the revolution of the earth around the sun. At night, time is marked by the sun's light reflected upon the moon, and navigators use constellations of stars (many of which are other suns) as a map and guide.

The lectionary readings for Epiphany Day focus on the dawning of God's glory in the incarnate Christ as sunlight. Isaiah 60:1–6 implores Christians to "arise, shine; for your light has come, and the glory of the LORD has risen upon you," and proceeds to describe the coming glory of Christ as the coming of the sun: Just as the sun provides an inexhaustible light for the earth, God's glory revealed in Christ will fill the entirety of the earth and eradicate its darkness. Just as the sun's brightness quells the clouds of depression, the glory of Christ will raise the spirits of the downtrodden, so that their hearts "shall thrill and rejoice." And just as the sun's light is accessible to anyone around the earth, the revelation of the light of Christ will open the door for all peoples, Jew and gentile alike, to experience God's glory. In the Epistle lection, Paul states explicitly that the coming of Jesus Christ has meant that the glory of God is now accessible to those all over the world, each receiving equally from this omnipresent and inexhaustible light: "The Gentiles have become fellow heirs, members of the same body, and sharers in the promise in Christ Jesus through the gospel" (Eph. 3:6).

Both the Isaiah and Psalter passages for Epiphany describe some of these fellow gentile heirs who will flock to the light of Christ: wealthy kings from faraway lands, as far as Arabia, Saba, and Sheba (Ps. 72:10–11; Isa. 60:3–4). The Gospel selection on this day highlights the fulfillment of these prophecies in the account of the three wise men (Matt. 2:1–12). Three wealthy kings from the East who embody the Isaian prophecies see a new star rising in the sky, and this new sun guides them to its resting point over the incarnate Son of God. The rising of the star of Bethlehem is the beginning of the fulfillment of Isaiah, for it is the first instance of the glory of God replacing the sun as the source of light and guidance. Jesus is the Son and the new sun who alters the ways in which we understand the cosmos and our place within it.

Gold

The term *glory* carries with it both receptive and responsive connotations: Beholding the glory of another can invite the recipient to give glory, to give honor, to the one revealed. The three wise men traverse the world under the guidance of the star of Bethlehem, and when they arrive under this new sun, they behold God's glory in the infant Christ. This encounter *with* God's glory naturally compels them to respond by *giving* glory to God. They do this by opening up their treasure chests to give frankincense, myrrh, and, above all, gold. Gold has been the most precious of metals in nearly all civilizations throughout human history. Yet, despite its near ubiquity as an expensive commodity, gold has remained limited in its utility. It is one of the softest metals in existence, useless for battle and building. Its value is instead derived from its scarcity and beauty. When sunlight strikes pure gold, it emits a radiance unlike any other found on earth. Gold naturally attracts the eyes, and so is used to ornament buildings or to accentuate human beauty when crafted into jewelry.

These unique qualities of gold make it an incredible gift, perhaps the most gifted item in all of human history. When someone gives a gift of gold, they are giving up something that is incredibly valuable yet has no utility. Oftentimes the best gifts have this combination of high cost and low utility. High-utility gifts, like a lawn mower, can often indicate a more transactional relationship. Low-cost gifts, like giving dandelions instead of roses, can often indicate a lack of value in a relationship. Contrary to these kinds of gifts, gold requires a high degree of financial sacrifice with little to no return benefit.

Gold is mentioned throughout Scripture as a special gift given in response to an encounter with God's glory. In giving gold, the wise men indicate that Jesus is the most precious person in their life. They are willing to sacrifice an extraordinary amount of time just to get close to Jesus, and they give the most expensive gift possible in response to simply being with Jesus. What's more, they receive nothing in return for their gift, as Mary and Joseph have little to offer. Instead, they give freely and abundantly; their only hope is that the sunlike glory of God revealed in Jesus might be reflected on the gold that they give.

Encountering Glory in the Church Today

Christians live out these lectionary readings first and foremost by ordering their lives, and their sense of time, around Jesus as new sun and guiding light. From the beginning, Christians changed their calendar to revolve around Jesus, marking the emergence of the star of Bethlehem as the first day of the new age, the "year of our Lord." Furthermore, Christians gathered on Sun-day, the first day of each week and the day specifically named for the sun: "Sunday, indeed, is the day on which we all hold our common assembly because it is the first day on which God, transforming the darkness and [prime] matter, created the world; and our Savior Jesus Christ arose from the dead on the same day."[1] The historic placement of altars facing east, and the practice of personal prayer facing east, also attest to this orientation of space and time around Jesus Christ: The rising of the sun in the morning directs our hearts and prayers upward to the new sun and only begotten Son of God.

Each Sunday, the glory of God rests on the church assembly, coming to stop above the gathering just like the star of Bethlehem, and Christians flock from all around town to bask in this radiance. In response, Christians are called to orient their personal calendars and schedules around this unique gathering. Work, rest, and vacations are to be squeezed in around Sunday worship, and never the other way around. As the wise men sacrificed months of their lives, as well as their bodily and financial security, to surround Jesus, Christians are invited to sacrifice time, energy, and even their own lives to be surrounded by the body of Christ.

Upon entrance into the church, Christians encounter the glory of God and respond in turn by giving glory to God. They do so in two significant ways. First, they heap praise and honor on the name of God with their voices in verbal responses and the singing of hymns. One of the most ancient antiphons is the Gloria Patri, which is often recited at the end of the Psalm readings: "Glory to the Father, and to the Son, and to the Holy Spirit: as it was in the beginning, is now, and will be forever. Amen." In addition to this antiphon, the church routinely sings the doxology Gloria in Excelsis, whose lyrics are taken directly from the chorus of angels who appear to announce the incarnate Jesus in the Christmas I lectionary readings (Luke 2:14). When Christians sing this hymn, their voices intertwine and intermix with this heavenly host of angels and archangels who glorify God in response to the manifestation of God's glory in Jesus Christ.

As the service progresses, Christians have an opportunity to give glory to God through the offering. The offering is an opportunity for Christians to open up their treasure chests and give back to God out of the abundance that God has given to them. A plate is passed around, and Christians drop their most valuable resources in, their monies intermingling with the offerings of the Magi at Bethlehem. Like with the wise men, the principal purpose of such an offering is purely to give back to God: We give not principally to pay a salary or fix a building, but first and foremost to give glory to God and to indicate that the worship of Jesus Christ is worth sacrificing the best of our time, money, and energy.

The glory of God is revealed in Jesus Christ, the light of the world. The birth of Jesus Christ inaugurates a new era, where the Sun of righteousness begins to shine over all the world. But this light has not shone on everyone, and human beings are still incapable, on their own merits, of fully encountering the glory revealed by the light of Christ. Full access to this glory must wait for the full disclosure of God's glory in Jesus's transfiguration on Mount Tabor and the invitation to participate in this glory when Christ descends on Mount Zion. In order to access the fullness of God's glory in Christ, Christians must confront their own sin so that the fullness of God may be made visible to them. For this reason, the lectionary, and the church year, progresses from the season of Epiphany to the season of Lent.

CHAPTER 3

REPENTANCE

Christ Crushes the Serpent

Ash Wednesday, Lent 1A, B, C, 4B, 4C, Advent 2A, 3C

Almighty God, whose blessed Son was led by the Spirit to be tempted by Satan: Come quickly to help us who are assaulted by many temptations; and, as you know the weaknesses of each of us, let each one find you mighty to save; through Jesus Christ your Son our Lord, who lives and reigns with you and the Holy Spirit, one God, now and for ever. Amen.

Collect for the First Sunday in Lent (2019 BCP)

CHRIST OUR LIGHT has come to fill the earth with God's glory, but his pure celestial brightness also illuminates the darkness of the human heart. As the church calendar moves from Epiphany to Lent, the lectionary readings transition from the revelation of God's glory to the need for human beings to acknowledge the ways in which their sin prevents this glory from reaching the soul.

Lent is a season of fasting and repentance in preparation for the events of Good Friday and Easter. Beginning on Ash Wednesday, and periodically throughout the various Lenten Sundays, the lectionary unfolds the complex relationship between temptation, sin, and its cure, a relationship that is anticipated in the middle portion of the Advent readings (2A, 3C). One symbol and two actions threaded through these lections aid in our understanding of this relationship: snakes, fasting, and repentance.

Snakes

The opening week of Lent (1A) details the first sins in human history, in which Adam and Eve succumb to temptation and eat from the tree of the knowledge of good and evil (Gen. 2:15–17; 3:1–7). Satan's chosen vessel for this temptation was a serpent, and snakes continue to be the preeminent symbol for evil and temptation throughout Scripture. The lectionary readings draw from a number of passages related to the symbol of the serpent in order to highlight the various ways that human beings are tempted to sin, as well as the dangers that come in refusing to acknowledge when one has succumbed to sin.

While the first Sunday of Lent for all three years addresses temptation through the Gospel account of Jesus's temptation in the wilderness (Matt. 4:1–11; Mark 1:9–15;

Luke 4:1–13), 1A draws out the connections between Jesus's temptation and the temptation of Adam and Eve. We see in the Genesis reading for this week the threefold temptation of Adam and Eve: They are tempted by gluttony to eat more fruit than they need, they are tempted by pride to "become like God," and finally they are tempted by desire to place their wants above obedience to God. It is this last temptation that tips Eve to sin, as she "desires" the tree with her eyes, then takes and eats of the forbidden fruit.

Genesis 2 depicts this first sin as an admixture of avarice and pride, stoked by temptation, and culminating in a desire to disobey God. This desire itself is sinful, with the ensuing words and actions a manifestation of a heart set on disobedience. When attempting to trace the genealogy of sin in the human heart, Christians have long taken their cue from this depiction. Some, like John Chrysostom, prioritize avarice, while others, such as Augustine, emphasize pride. But whichever is prioritized, all agree that the cure must address the entirety of sin in all its complexity.

The Gospel readings from all three weeks of the first Sunday of Lent detail Jesus's duel with the devil and reveal how his temptations mirror the temptations of Adam and Eve in Eden: He is tempted by gluttony (turning stones to bread), by pride (letting angels break his fall), and by desire (to rule over the nations). As we'll see below, in resisting these temptations, Jesus defeats the serpent, allowing human beings to resist the devil to this day.

While the serpent is the preeminent symbol of temptation in Scripture, its venom is associated with the consequences for those who have succumbed to temptation: death. The readings for Lent 4B draw out this association between death, sin, and the serpent's venom. The first reading for this day (Num. 21:4–9) chronicles the wilderness complaints of the Israelites, who pine for the creature comforts they left behind in Egypt. As a result of this complaint, venomous snakes emerge to bite and kill. Death is the result of these snakebites, and venom remains a symbol of those who have succumbed to the temptation of the serpent. Just as physical death is the result of a venomous snakebite, physical and spiritual death awaits all those who succumb to temptation and refuse to repent.

Together, these serpentine passages highlight how temptation often comes in the form of a mental image. Satan conjures up images to implant in the human mind, with the hopes that such images will take root and lead to a desire for disobedience. In Eden, Adam and Eve were tempted by images of the future: a life of comfort, power, and autonomy. Likewise, Jesus was tempted by images of future satiation and earthly splendor. In the wilderness, the Israelites were tempted by images of the past: Satan uses nostalgia as the principal vehicle of temptation, conjuring images of past comfort, the "fleshpots of Egypt" (Exod. 16:3). Satan intentionally omits images of past servitude from these temptations in hopes that Israel will forget their past hardships and fixate only on their present discomforts. Temptation often follows similar contours today. The young, like Adam and Eve, are tempted by future hopes and dreams. The middle-aged and old are tempted by the past, by the roads not traveled and the allure of an easier life. Both temptations attempt to persuade Christians to forget the ways that God has blessed their lives and convince them that true happiness can come only if they abandon their trust in God.

Fasting

The lectionary readings describe temptation as a fact of life: All human beings can and will be tempted as the result of living in a sinful world. Holiness does not inoculate one against temptation—the Gospel passages for Lent 1 show the sinless and perfectly holy Son of God enduring immense temptation. But the lectionary readings also show a way to bolster one's defenses, as well as a way to seek a cure once one has succumbed to temptation. This protection comes through fasting in and through Jesus Christ.

The centrality of fasting is seen in the run-up to Jesus's duel with Satan on the mountain. Jesus goes out to the wilderness, the place where the Israelites were attacked by serpents for their failure, and fasts for forty days. Satan views this fast as a weakness and tempts Jesus to prematurely end his fast by turning stones to bread. However, this fast is not a weakness but a strength, providing Jesus with a robust vantage point through which to resist the devil and his wiles.

Fasting likewise is meant to strengthen Christians to fight the temptations of the serpent. It makes us alert to the ways in which the material things of the world can compete with the primary goal of worshiping God. Within a few hours of fasting, we realize the pull of the belly and the temptation to place its satiation above the glory of God. But Christians can conquer this initial temptation by drawing on the strength of the fast of Jesus. When we do, we discover that fasting frees us from a reliance on material things, enabling our hearts to focus on spiritual concerns. In fasting, the eyes of the soul are lifted upward from the stuff of the world to the stuff of heaven.

The lectionary for the first week of Lent teaches us that fasting is the way to fight temptation, but it is a specific kind of fasting. Fasting on its own does not bring about holiness. One can, after all, fast for health reasons, or fast for vanity's sake. It is only fasting in and through the fast of Jesus that provides Christians the strength to fight the serpent, since Jesus alone has the power to place his hands over the adder's den and subdue the snake (Isa. 11:8, Advent 2A). In the Gospel reading from Lent 4B, Jesus directly quotes the passage from Numbers concerning Moses and the bronze serpent: "Just as Moses lifted up the serpent in the wilderness, so must the Son of Man be lifted up" (John 3:14). According to Jesus, the Israelites should have seen their lack of food and water as an opportunity to fast and draw on God to fight temptation. After they succumbed to temptation and to the venom of the snakes, God provided a way for them to be healed. They were invited to see their hunger as a kind of fast and look to the wooden staff of Moses to be healed. In so doing, they were in fact lifting their eyes upward to the wood of the cross, drawing their strength from the crucified Christ. Just as Jesus conquered Satan when he was lifted up on the wood of the cross, Moses conquered Satan when he lifted this wood up in the desert. When we fast, in turn, we are called to turn our eyes upon Jesus and the cross to strengthen us and protect us from temptation.

The readings from Ash Wednesday further unpack Christians' need for fasting in the name of Jesus. Isaiah 58 criticizes all fasting done for selfish interests. Instead, in fasting we are called to humble ourselves and to call upon the name of Jesus to fight temptation for us. Here, however, there can arise an even subtler temptation: Our humility itself can become a temptation to pride. In our zeal for humility, we can easily strive to become someone who takes pride in being humble, fasting in order to be known as a pious person who fasts. For this reason, Jesus further unfurls the true meaning of the fast, cautioning against both pride and false humility: When we fast, we are called to fast in secret, putting oil on our head to give the appearance of health (Matt. 6:16–18, Ash Wednesday).

Repentance

Many of the readings from Ash Wednesday focus on the ways in which human beings are tempted to sin, and the ways that we can fight temptation by participating in the fast of Jesus Christ. But what happens when we succumb to temptation? The lectionary readings for Advent and Lent call on Christians not only to resist temptation, but to humbly repent of our sins whenever we are bitten by the venomous snake. The season of Advent functions in many ways as a kind of mini-Lent—it too arose out of a period of fasting and repentance in anticipation of the coming of Christ. And so many of the Advent readings touch on the need for repentance, particularly those weeks that focus on the ministry of John the Baptist (Matt. 3:1–12, Advent 2A; Luke 3:7–18, Advent 3C). The readings from Advent 2A in particular highlight the Baptist's ministry of repentance. John calls the Pharisees and Sadducees a "brood of vipers" and warns them that their genetic history as children of Abraham will not protect them from the wrath to come (Matt. 3:7; Luke 3:7). John is in effect stating that, without true repentance, we do not realize that we have ingested the poison. Left untreated, we will become snakes ourselves, doing the work and will of Satan.

True repentance, done with a full acceptance of the wrath that comes to the unrepentant, is required of all of those who have been bitten by the serpent. We are given a model of what true repentance looks like in the great parable of the prodigal son (Luke 15:11–32, Lent 4C). The wayward son takes his inheritance and squanders it in a foreign country. But after the fortune is exhausted, he finds himself starving, knee-deep in pig slop. Pigs are symbols of dissipation and degradation, and Jesus even uses pigs as vessels for exorcised demons (Matt. 8:28–34). The prodigal son's descent into the company of pigs indicates that he has both been surrounded by demons and succumbed to them.

The story of the prodigal reenacts the primordial sin: A human being is tempted by images of a future life of satiation and prideful independence, succumbing in a great act of disobedience against their father. Like Adam and Eve, the son receives a life of hardship in the wilderness as a result of this disobedience. But while starving in the sty, the prodigal son discovers the fast. As his stomach growls, he realizes the words of Jesus that "man does not live on bread alone" and decides to fully repent and return to his father. He leaves his father's house as a child of the old Adam, but it is through the fast of the new Adam that he finds his way home.

The prodigal's full repentance embodies that of the psalm for Lent 4C: "While I held my tongue, my bones withered away, because of my groaning all day long. . . . Then I acknowledged my sin to you, and did not conceal my guilt. I said, 'I will confess my transgressions to the Lord.' Then you forgave me the guilt of my sin" (32:5–6). This psalm, coupled with the prodigal son parable, shows what true repentance looks like. In repentance we acknowledge failure—our failure to trust in God, failure to resist the lure of gluttony and avarice. Repentance is open, honest, and guileless. But it is not enough. In the end, repentance still requires the embrace of the merciful Father to bring reconciliation and restoration. Such mercy comes through the sacrifice of Jesus, which is addressed in our next chapter.

Fasting and Repentance in the Church Today

Temptation is a fact of life for all human beings who live "east of Eden." As the lectionary readings for Lent show, the perfect holiness of Jesus Christ did not inoculate him against temptation. But we are now able to resist the temptation of the serpent by drawing on the power of Jesus Christ, and our resistance is bolstered when we fast in the name of Jesus Christ. Jesus "showed to us the power veiled in the fast, conquering all, whereby one conquers that one who by fruit conquered Adam and devoured him."[1] Fasting has been a feature of the Christian life from the very beginning, and the church continues to call forth days of fasting in order to train its members to fight temptation. Traditionally, Fridays in Lent have been reserved as the most prominent time for a churchwide fast. When Christians fast on Fridays, they lift their eyes up to the wood of the cross that is raised on Good Friday, seeing in the crucified Christ the one who conquered the serpent. In so doing, they draw their strength from Jesus to fight temptation.

One important and often neglected tradition has been the practice of fasting in the morning before receiving the Eucharist. These microfasts provide an opportunity to experience the fast of Jesus and his defeat of Satan in the desert. Just as Jesus removed himself from the busy world to fast in the wilderness, Christians remove themselves from their busy lives by entering the church. With empty stomachs they hear the words of Scripture read out loud in the congregation, and experience in their body the truth that a hungry Jesus pronounced to the tempter: "Man shall not live by bread alone, but by every word that comes from the mouth of God" (Matt. 4:4 ESV). By fasting and hearing God's Word, we learn to rely on the immaterial words of Scripture as true sustenance. As the worship service progresses, we find ourselves less attached to the things below and our hearts more fixed on the things above. We find that the Word of God is capable of defeating the serpents tempting our souls. And, just as Jesus's defeat of Satan ended with him resting with angels, we end our fast by resting with angels and archangels as we enjoy our heavenly feast of bread and wine.

But before this heavenly feast, Christians are granted an opportunity to fully repent of the ways that they have succumbed to temptation throughout the week through a time of corporate confession. The written confession functions as a kind of sin diagnostic, poking and prodding the soul to unearth all of the ways in which we have sinned in thought, word, deed, action, and inaction. The goal is guileless confession, to see ourselves as sinners in slop whose souls are constantly bothered by the piglike squeals of demons. As the prodigal son realized his sin, embraced the fast, and pleaded for mercy from his father, we are invited to fast before church and realize our own sin in confession, pleading for mercy by shouting "Kyrie Eleison": "Lord, have mercy."

But confession is incomplete on its own, since confession itself cannot bring about reconciliation. As we discover whenever we have harmed other people, in order for reconciliation to occur, those hurt must choose to forgive our offenses. The prodigal son was not reconciled solely through his penitence; he had to be received and embraced by his forgiving father. For our relationship with God, reconciliation can only come when the damage caused by our sin is addressed and when the aggrieved Father chooses to welcome us back with an embrace. And so the lectionary readings throughout Lent continue by showing Christians the kind of sacrifice required to address sin and the specific ways God seeks to welcome back his lost children into his house.

CHAPTER 4

SACRIFICE

Christ's Blood Shed for Us

Holy Week, Proper 19A, 20A, Palm Sunday A, B, C

O God, by the passion of your blessed Son you made an instrument of shameful death to be for us the means of life: Grant us so to glory in the cross of Christ, that we may gladly suffer shame and loss for the sake of your Son our Savior Jesus Christ; who lives and reigns with you and the Holy Spirit, one God, for ever and ever. Amen.

Collect for Tuesday of Holy Week (1979 BCP)

THE LECTIONARY readings during most of Lent say comparatively little about the cross and resurrection; instead, the seven days of Holy Week are used to explain these sacred mysteries. Because of the importance of the cross of Christ, the readings throughout Holy Week serve as a kind of extended commentary and explanation of its significance. The passion accounts from the Gospels provide the narrative, while Isaiah, the Psalms, and Hebrews unpack the depths of this narrative. Isaiah in particular functions as a kind of fifth Gospel, a commentary on the Good News disclosed on Good Friday. Here it is good to be reminded of the notion of sacred time in Scripture—the book of Isaiah, though written before the Gospels, is actually a commentary on the Gospels, not merely a series of predictions about Jesus.

The lections selected for Holy Week focus specifically on the theme of the cross as sacrifice, with the concomitant symbols of lamb, blood, and curtain developing this central theme. Together, these symbols help us understand who is sacrificed (Jesus, the Lamb of God), where he is sacrificed (in the heavenly temple), and why he is sacrificed (for the reestablishment of intimacy with God).

Lamb

The damaging effects of sin are complex and far-reaching, infecting both individuals and relationships. Sin manifests itself in physical, psychological, and spiritual harm, generating countless victims and corroding the souls of its perpetrators. Civilizations have long grappled with the challenge of remedying the effects of sin and expiating the guilt of sin from the community. Scapegoating, the process by which the sins of a community are cast upon an individual who is subsequently killed or expelled, is perhaps the most common way in which societies deal with the complexity of sin.

In Scripture, lambs are the preeminent symbols of the process whereby sin is addressed and expunged. In certain Old Testament sacrifices, the sins of the individual or community were ceremonially placed on a lamb, and its life was then taken in order to remove the guilt of the sinner. The death of the lamb spared the sinful person. Lambs were particularly important animals for this sacrifice due to their innocence. They are pleasant and peaceful animals. Even as they are being slaughtered, they offer up no resistance, refusing to fight back.

But these sacrifices offered only a temporary reprieve from the guilt of sin. An animal was not a sufficient sacrifice for the totality of human sin, whether individually or collectively. As such, the lamb was also a sign that a greater, complete sacrifice was needed to bring about the remediation of the sin of the world. The reading from Isaiah on Good Friday describes the death of Jesus as this complete and perfect sacrifice. According to Isaiah, Jesus is the "lamb that is led to the slaughter" (53:7), and Isaiah continues throughout this Good Friday reading to chronicle the numerous maladies that are visited on Jesus during his passion. Jesus is despised and rejected, he bears infirmities, and he is wounded and afflicted by others. And yet, through all of it, Isaiah declares that Jesus remains silent, accepting this unjust punishment. Like a lamb, he refuses to fight back, willfully accepting this punishment on behalf of humanity. The Isaiah reading from Holy

Wednesday furthers this point. Here, Jesus cries out: "I gave my back to those who struck me, and my cheeks to those who pulled out the beard; I did not hide my face from insult and spitting" (50:6).

Isaiah shows that, as the lamb that takes on himself the entirety of human sin, Jesus had to endure the full weight of sin in all of the manifold and intricate ways it manifests itself in the world. Likewise, the Hebrews reading from Holy Wednesday exhorts the church to "consider him who endured such hostility against himself from sinners" (Heb. 12:3). These readings prepare the church to experience these hostilities as they walk with Christ through the events leading up to his death on Good Friday. In the Gospel reading for Good Friday (as well as the Passion Narratives for Palm Sunday), we find that Jesus is abused and afflicted in every way imaginable. He is abandoned by his friends, abused by soldiers, mocked by the crowd, and used by Pontius Pilate as a political pawn (John 18:1–19:42). Every kind of person—rich and poor, Jew and gentile, working class and ruling class—sins against Jesus in every way imaginable. Good Friday pairs John's Passion Narrative with Psalm 22, which are the words of Christ on the cross lamenting the great afflictions imputed on him: his thirst, his abandonment, and the mockeries hurled at him.

While the breadth of human sin is shown in these various condemnations of Jesus, the depth of human sin is detailed throughout Holy Week in the betrayal of Jesus by Judas Iscariot. Monday of Holy Week depicts the anointing of Jesus by Mary of Bethany, an extraordinary act of worship that elicits contempt from an onlooking Judas (John 12:1–11). Herein lie the seeds of betrayal: Judas is unwilling to accept Jesus as Lord and God and thus views the opulent worship of Jesus as a colossal waste of time and money. Then, on the Wednesday of Holy Week (Betrayal, or "Spy" Wednesday), we see Jesus during the Last Supper disclose to his disciples that "one of you will betray me" (13:21). The scene ends with Judas eating the dipped piece of bread, and with it ingesting the venom of Satan. The full manifestation of Judas's betrayal is shown on Good Friday, when he hands Jesus over to the authorities for thirty pieces of silver (18:1–6).

The lectionary readings focus on Judas in order to highlight betrayal as a particularly deep and painful display of sin. Betrayal leverages the intimacy of relationships for selfish gain. It is not the act of a random acquaintance but of a close friend. The depiction of the Last Supper drawn from Wednesday and Thursday in Holy Week portrays vividly this relationship between intimacy and betrayal. The Supper is a deeply intimate moment between Christ and his followers, which culminates in a vulnerable act of foot washing and the bestowal of a new commandment of love. And yet these tender, loving moments are tinged with tension, as the reader knows that Judas will soon leverage his intimate access to Jesus for the sake of vanity and profit. The revelation that Jesus knows this will happen, yet nonetheless carries on with the foot washing, demonstrates his willful acceptance to take upon himself sin in all its bitter permutations.

Blood

Blood is a sign of both life and death. On the one hand, it is a source of human life: The constant pumping of blood through the heart sustains and invigorates animal existence. On the other hand, the loss of blood indicates a loss of life, a sign that death is close at hand. As a result of sin, human beings are unmoored from their source of permanent life, and their bodies are subject to decay and death. Sin, in effect, bursts open the human body: Blood seeps through wounded and frayed skin and dissolves after life expires.

In forming the people of God out of Abraham, God begins a long process of educating Israel on the connection between sin and death through the symbol of blood. Blood reminds Israel of the gravity of human sin, which leads to death. But in the shedding of animal blood, God reveals that another living being is able to bear the consequences of sin on behalf of humanity. And so blood also carries with it a sign of God's mercy. The lectionary's inclusion of the sacrifice of Isaac in the Easter Vigil service provides the most vivid account of blood shed as a sign of God's mercy (Gen. 22:1–18). Here, Abraham is spared the slaying of his son with a knife and is provided a ram to slaughter in Isaac's place. In this account, Abraham learns the gravity of human sin—that all human beings, even children, will lose their blood due to sin. Yet Abraham also learns through the thorn-enclosed ram that God will provide a merciful reprieve from death through the shedding of innocent blood.

Holy Week takes up this theme of blood as both a sign of the gravity of human sin and a mark of the extraordinary mercy of God, showing how the cross fulfills what is prefigured in the Old Testament. The Hebrews reading from Holy Monday shows that the blood of Christ is superior to the blood of animals, as it is capable of providing complete and eternal redemption of the soul (9:11–15). Maundy Thursday pairs the institution of the Passover meal in Exodus with its fulfillment in the Last Supper: Just as the blood of the lamb smeared on posts physically protected Israel from death in Egypt, so does the blood of the Lamb of God received in the wine of the Eucharist protect Christians from eternal death (Exod. 12:1–14; John 13:1–17, 31–35).

The mercy of God is manifested most vividly in the final scene of the passion of Christ read on Good Friday (John 18:1–19:42). Here, soldiers pierce the side of Jesus shortly after his death, and blood and water spill out. At the sight of this blood, the very life of Jesus poured out, Christians learn that the Lamb of God has given up his life for their sake. The blood and water that pour forth also indicate that the sacraments of baptism and communion continue to nourish the church, reminding Christians of the permanence of Christ's sacrifice. The lectionary readings are ordered so as to enable Christians to draw the connection between the institution of the Eucharist on Maundy Thursday and the sacrifice of Christ on Good Friday. In partaking of the cup of wine, Christians remember the blood shed on the cross and "proclaim the Lord's death until he comes" (1 Cor. 11:26, Maundy Thursday).

Augustine sums up this connection perfectly: "Here was opened the gate of life from which the sacraments of the church flowed without which we cannot enter into that life that is the true life: 'And there came out blood and water.' That blood was shed for the remission of sins. That water tempers the cup of salvation."[1]

Curtain

The symbols of lamb and blood show that the sacrifice of Christ on the cross was an extraordinary act of love and a demonstration of the extraordinary mercy of God. What is accomplished in this great sacrificial outpouring of love is intimated by Jesus at the Last Supper: "This is my blood of the covenant, which is poured out for many for the forgiveness of sins" (Matt. 26:28). Jesus obediently and willfully endures the sins of the world and spills his blood to remedy the consequences of sin, and these acts enable a restoration of humanity's relationship to God. The lectionary readings for Holy Week describe this restored relationship through the image of the curtain. In the Old Testament temple, curtains separated the Israelites from the Holy of Holies, the place of God's presence and the place of intimacy with God. The curtain was a sign that, no matter how many animals were sacrificed, full intimacy with God was not possible because of the enduring issue of sin. However, since Jesus's death is the full, complete, once-for-all sacrifice for human sin, full intimacy with God can now be restored.

On Holy Monday, the Letter to the Hebrews reveals the stunning reality of Calvary—in ascending Mount Golgotha, Jesus ascends into the heavenly temple, shedding his blood before the Father to provide the perfect, once-for-all sacrifice for the forgiveness of sins (9:11–15). This sacrifice was performed outside of time, and is thus capable of forgiving all sins, past, present, and future. The selection from Hebrews on Good Friday states that Jesus's body, his flesh, was the curtain, and when it was torn open, it opened up a path for humanity to enter into God's presence: "Therefore, brothers, since we have confidence to enter the holy places by the blood of Jesus, by the new and living way that he opened for us through the curtain, that is, through his flesh," we can now "draw near with a true heart in full assurance of faith" (10:19–20, 22 ESV).

The passion readings from Matthew and Mark (Palm Sunday, years A and B) dramatically depict the reconciliation between God and humanity made available through the cross of Christ through the tearing of the temple curtain at the moment of Christ's death (Matt. 27:51; Mark 15:38). The tearing of the curtain and the tearing of the flesh of Jesus in these accounts show that the barrier of sin that separates us from God is now eradicated.

Sacrifice in the Church Today

The cross of Christ enables the forgiveness of sins and the reconciliation of humankind to God, and its centrality to the Christian faith is emphasized in nearly every aspect of Christian worship. When Christians make the sign of the cross on their bodies throughout a worship service, and when they mark their head, lips, and heart before the Gospel reading, they participate in both the smearing of Christ's blood on the cross and the smearing of the doorposts with the blood of the lamb at Passover.[2] As hand touches head and heart, they feel the blood of the lamb shed for them and are reminded of the deep mercy of God.

This experience of mercy culminates in the singing of the Agnus Dei during the Eucharist celebration. In this melodic request that the "Lamb of God who takes away the sin of the world, have mercy on us," the church knows that the sins she confessed earlier in the service are now fully forgiven. Whether its members have denied Jesus like Peter, or placed their careers above Jesus like Pilate, or mocked him like the soldiers, they now know that through true confession these sins are imputed to the Lamb of God. In chanting the Agnus Dei, they experience in their hearts the reality that their sins are not more than the Lamb of God can bear.

Shortly after reciting this antiphon, the priest declares to the assembly that "Christ our Passover is sacrificed for us."[3] Here the church experiences the "once for all" of the cross that the author of Hebrews elucidates: Christ's blood, shed in the heavenly temple, completely forgives all sins past, present, and future. Because the death of Jesus Christ takes place in sacred time, Christians experience in the Eucharistic celebration his sacrifice in the present tense: Christ shed his blood for the onlookers two thousand years ago, but he also shed his blood for *me, right now*.

After the church responds to the words of the priest, "Therefore let us keep the feast, alleluia," the priest comes down from the altar, and the congregation ascends to receive the bread and wine. Unlike those who worshiped in the temple, whose access was restricted by a curtain, Christians are able to approach the altar without impediment. Heaven is opened, and they are invited to approach their loving God with "childlike trust,"[4] heeding the words of Hebrews as they "approach with a true heart in full assurance of faith" (10:19). As they ingest the communion wine-turned-blood of Christ, the certainty of the mercy of God, poured out through the veins of the Lamb, is felt sharply in their bellies.

The forgiveness that is ingested in the stomach is meant to be converted into calories, energy to be expended to extend forgiveness to others. As Christians are reconciled to God through the blood of Christ, they are in turn called to extend this forgiveness to others. While the lectionary for Holy Week focuses on the initiative of God in forgiving human beings, it devotes specific weeks during Ordinary Time to detailing the ways in which Christians are to likewise extend forgiveness to others. Proper 19A connects Jesus's teaching to forgive seventy-seven times and his parable of the wicked slave (Matt. 18:21–35) to the Genesis account of Joseph extending forgiveness to his brothers (Gen. 50:15–21). In reading these passages together, Christians are presented with a choice: Either they can refuse to extend the mercy of God like the wicked slave, or they can share in the extension of God's mercy through Joseph.

While these passages invite Christians to extend God's mercy, the readings for Proper 20A invite Christians to be glad and delight in the extension of God's mercy even to those whom they perceive as undeserving. The lections combine the reflections of Jonah 3:10–4:11 with Jesus's parable of the merciful landowner in Matthew 20:1–16. Just like the readings for Proper 19A, the lections for 20A invite Christians to make a choice: Will they stand with Jonah in begrudging the shedding of God's mercy on the Ninevites, or will they delight with the landowner who generously bestows the riches of God's mercy even on those who have done little to earn it?

The worship service itself is a gathering meant to embody Christ's mercy through the forgiving relationships formed between the members of the church. The church is composed of members committed to Christ and to each other, and who are thus committed to forgiving each other for their trespasses. This is seen most vividly in the passing of the peace, which was originally intended as a time for Christians to repair any lingering conflicts before gathering around the communion table. In setting aside time each Sunday for members to extend forgiveness to each other, the church lives out the command of Jesus to extend mercy to the seventy-seventh time. Once reconciled, the church can then unite to drink from the common cup of salvation, receiving in their bellies the blood of God's mercy.

The first five days of Holy Week chronicle the events leading up to the cross of Christ and expand on its significance for humankind. But while the blood of the Lamb shed for Christians on Good Friday enables the forgiveness of sins, the ultimate consequence of sin—death—is yet to be conquered. For this reason, Holy Week continues with the descent of Christ into death on Holy Saturday and his resurrection on Easter Sunday.

CHAPTER 5

RESURRECTION

Christ the Firstfruits

Holy Saturday, Easter Vigil, Easter Principal and Evening, Easter 3B, 3C, 4C, 5C, 6C

O God, who by the glorious resurrection of your Son Jesus Christ destroyed death and brought life and immortality to light: Grant that we, who have been raised with him, may abide in his presence and rejoice in the hope of eternal glory; through Jesus Christ our Lord, to whom, with you and the Holy Spirit, be dominion and praise for ever and ever. Amen.

Collect for Tuesday of Easter Week (1979 BCP)

WHILE GOOD FRIDAY focuses on the events up to and including the crucifixion of Jesus, its significance cannot be grasped in isolation from his burial and resurrection in the ensuing days. The lectionary readings for Holy Saturday, Easter, and the weeks that follow present a collection of symbols that unpack the significance of Jesus's death and resurrection: Jesus's death and burial are examined through the symbols of darkness, rock, and linen, and Jesus's resurrection is explored through the empty tomb and its location in a garden and on a mountain.

Death, Darkness, and Descent

Advent uses the symbol of darkness to depict the chaos and disorder that exists in a still-sinful world. But darkness is also a symbol of the *telos* (the final end) of sin, which is death. Death is the cessation of life, a loss of our ability to think, act, and will. Before contemplating what will occur in the afterlife, one must reckon with the immediate deprivation of agency that comes in death, where our ability to see, together with all of our faculties, will diminish and extinguish into darkness. The Old Testament lection from Holy Saturday (Lam. 3:1–9, 19–24) describes the inevitability of death for all human beings. All human flesh is corrupted by sin and deserves the rod of God's wrath. Because of sin, all human flesh is subject to decay, with human life ending with a descent into darkness. The culmination of this banishment comes in death, where one's agency is extinguished, blocked by "hewn stones" (v. 9).

The Epistle reading from 1 Peter 4:1–8 is paired with this passage in order to show that Jesus Christ took upon himself the descent into darkness described in Lamentations. Peter describes the death of Jesus as a suffering that occurred "in the flesh" (v. 1). Though Jesus himself was without sin, he took the entirety of human sin upon his flesh, and it is that sin (not the person of Jesus) that bears the wrath of God described in Lamentations. The Gospel passage from Holy Saturday further chronicles Jesus's descent to darkness, as he is covered in a clean linen cloth and laid in an empty tomb that is sealed with hewn stone.

Darkness descending into a pit sealed by stone. The lectionary readings for Holy Saturday use these symbols of darkness and stone in order to emphasize the real and complete death of Jesus Christ. Jesus's divinity did not prevent him from experiencing a fully human death. His death on the cross was not a kind of stage death, a drama performed before our eyes for pedagogical purposes. Rather, it was a real descent into the abyss, the same descent experienced by all human beings since the fall of Adam and Eve.

Jesus fully descends into the darkness so that he might fully conquer death. According to Peter, Jesus descends to Sheol not in defeat but in victory, proclaiming the gospel to the dead he encounters there "so that, though they had been judged in the flesh as everyone is judged, they might live in the spirit as God does" (1 Pet. 4:6). In Jesus, God has entered the place of the dead and broken the bonds of hell. Satan's strength is no match for the Son of God, and the heavy chains of death are not strong enough to contain Jesus. What appeared on Good Friday to be a victory *for* Satan and death is now revealed to be the victory of God *over* Satan and death.

Tomb, Rock, and Linen

Three related symbols from Holy Saturday and Easter Sunday help us understand the magnitude of this victory over death accomplished through the resurrection of Christ: the empty tomb, the rock, and the linen clothes. On Holy Saturday, the Gospel account details the preparation and wrapping of Jesus's body in clean linen, emphasizing that he was laid in a "new tomb," one that did not house any other dead (Matt. 27:57–66). In addition, a stone was rolled over the entrance to prevent theft of the body. Then, on Easter Sunday, Matthew describes an angel moving the stone away, with Mary Magdelene and Mary witnessing an empty tomb and the discarded linen.

These symbols point to the reality of the resurrection of Christ as an objective event within human history. Unlike the foundational myths and ecstatic visions that ground the multitude of world religions, Christianity is grounded in an objective event that occurred in time, one that was subject to verification by the world. The difficulty of moving a large stone proves that Jesus's body was not stolen. The newness of the tomb shows that no one but Jesus could have emerged. The presence of linen shows that it is the same body of the crucified Christ that arose from this tomb.

The resurrection of Christ was a flesh and blood occurrence that took place in real time and is the cornerstone of Christian faith. As Paul states, "If Christ has not been raised, our preaching is useless and so is your faith" (1 Cor. 15:14 NIV). The Psalm selection for Easter Sunday emphasizes this point: The rock of the resurrection is the chief cornerstone, the grounds of Christian faith, and at the same time it is the principal stumbling block for those who refuse to believe (Ps. 118:22–24). There is a persistent temptation to treat the resurrection as a purely mythical event that is leveraged as a vehicle to ascend to a higher immaterial plane. This temptation is not just reserved for mystics; it manifests itself in a kind of popular religious pluralism common among many Christians today. Here, the resurrected Christ illuminates just one of many paths to God, a helpful but inessential gateway to a higher deity. Such understandings reject the claims of the resurrection as the cornerstone of faith—that it is God that is encountered in flesh and blood, God that is seen, touched, and embraced.

The Transfigured Body, the Garden, and the Mountain

While we see in the symbols of stone and tomb a resurrection that is a real, objective victory over death, the resurrection is also the "firstfruits" of new, eternal life that is now made possible through Christ Jesus. It is the first sign of what will be completed in the book of Revelation: Sin will be eradicated from earth, and heaven and earth will merge. We see this most fully in the resurrected body of Jesus. In the transfigured Jesus, heaven and earth are fully joined together. On the one hand, the resurrected Jesus is flesh and bone—the disciples grasp at his feet, and Mary Magdalene embraces him. All of his earthly body is incorporated in his resurrected body; "nothing is sloughed off; nothing left behind as inessential."[1] On the other hand, Jesus's transfigured, resurrected body bears the marks of heaven. The resurrected Christ transcends space and time, appearing and disappearing and entering through locked doors.

We see both the earthly and heavenly reality of Christ's resurrected body most clearly in the readings for Easter 3B. We learn from these passages that Jesus's resurrection was not an escape from the body but a *saturation* of the human body by the divine light of God's glory. In the Gospel passage, Jesus appears out of nowhere and is presumed to be a ghost, but he invites his disciples to embrace him, and he eats a piece of fish to reveal his full humanity (Luke 24:36–48). The Epistle reading declares that those who believe in the resurrected Christ will also share in this transfigured state: "What we do know is this: when he is revealed, we will be like him, for we will see him as he is" (1 John 3:2). At their death, Christians will not escape the material world but be resurrected in Christ, their bodies receiving their true fulfillment as bearers of the glory of God.

The Gospel readings for Easter focus specifically on the resurrected body of Christ as the firstfruits of a future resurrection for Christians (1 Cor. 15:19–26, Easter Principal C), but they also describe the specific location where this resurrection will take place: the eschatological Mount Zion. Two key symbols from Holy Saturday—garden and mountain—are given to elaborate on this heavenly destination. John 19:41 describes the location of Jesus's tomb as "a garden in the place where he was crucified." That place, as described on Good Friday, was Mount Golgotha (John 19:17). Hence, the resurrection of Jesus Christ, the firstfruits of new creation, begins in a garden on a mountain.

Mountains are the places in Scripture where human beings encounter God's glory, a kind of merging point between the human and divine. Ezekiel 28:13–14 describes Eden as a mountain where God created and placed Adam. The mountaintop garden on Eden was an intimate meeting place for Adam and Eve with God, where they encountered God's glory.[2] But the great severing of humankind from God occurred in this garden when Adam and Eve ate of the fruit and committed the first sin. The consequence of that sin was banishment from the mountain. Now, access to the mountain has been opened through the side of Jesus, and the resurrected body of Jesus is the first sign of what it will be like for human flesh to be fully with God once again. The lectionary readings for Easter thus seek to show how Jesus opens a way back to the mountain through images that remind us of our original home on Mount Eden. The placing of the body of Jesus in a garden shows us that Jesus has come to reverse the curse of Adam: As our fall from the mountain began in a garden, our return to the mountain begins in a garden. Upon first seeing the resurrected Jesus, Mary Magdalene refers to him as a "gardener," a sign that Jesus is the new Adam, the first gardener of Mount Zion.

The Old Testament readings throughout the Easter season are meant to elaborate on Mount Zion as the location of resurrected humanity. Jeremiah 31:1–6 (Easter Principal A) describes Mount Zion as a place of everlasting love, with garden-like vineyards that yield perfect and abundant fruit. Isaiah 25:6–9 (Easter Evening A) describes Mount Zion as a place untouched by death and marked by joyful feasting. Finally, the lectionary readings for year C of the Easter season incorporate key chapters from Revelation that further describe life on Zion: Death will be no more (Rev. 21:1–6, 5C), and the glory of God will fill all of creation (Rev. 21:10, 22–22:5, 6C). These passages show how the merger of heaven and earth made visible in the transfigured body of the resurrected Christ will be brought to its completion on Mount Zion, as all of faithful humanity and all of creation are illuminated by and radiate the glory of God.

While the readings for Easter primarily show how the gates of Mount Zion are opened by the resurrected Christ, the lectionary readings for year C of the Easter season describe the quality of life on Zion through the image of the feast. Readings from the Prophets and Revelation describe Mount Zion as a place free of hunger (Rev. 7:9–17, 4C), with a heavenly abundance, providing an everlasting feast of fine wine and rich food (Isa. 25:6–9, Easter Evening). These festive images correspond with the inclusion of the Gospel account of Jesus's final meal with his disciples in John 21:1–19 (Easter 3C). In this final act before his ascension, Jesus brings about a miraculous catch of fish for his disciples and prepares for them a final meal of bread and fish.[3]

In providing a superabundance of bread and fish, Jesus thus provides a second Eucharistic meal for his disciples, the first since the Last Supper. While the first Eucharist testified to his death on the cross, this second Eucharist testifies to his resurrection. It is a final feast that anticipates the eternal feast that the disciples will share with him on Mount Zion. This joyful, serene, and intimate meal with Jesus reminds the disciples that full intimacy with the resurrected Christ will be waiting for them when they rise at the last day.

Death and Resurrection in the Church Today

In the weekly celebration of the Eucharist, Christians are invited to experience the burial and resurrection of Jesus Christ and anticipate the fullness of new creation that began on Easter. The Eucharistic meal begins with death, as a clean linen cloth is placed on the altar, followed by bread and wine. Dead elements: Grain fallen from chaff and grapes ripped from a vine are carefully placed on linen, just as Christ's fallen body was placed on clean wrappings for burial. In this preparatory act, the church is reminded of the real death of Jesus Christ and is invited yet again to affirm their faith in his resurrection. For without the resurrection, the bread and wine would remain in their dead state, unable to provide spiritual nourishment. As the Eucharistic service continues, the pastor exhorts the church to "profess the mystery of faith: Christ has died, Christ is risen, Christ will come again." In so doing, the assembly declares their belief that God can raise the dead and that God can bring about life through dead wheat and pressed grapes.

Immediately after this declaration, the pastor calls on the Holy Spirit to bring heaven down upon these gifts, enabling them to become the bread of heaven and the cup of salvation. As Christ's resurrected body unites heaven and earth, the Eucharistic celebration becomes a uniting of heaven and earth as the bread and wine are received in faith. Christians are afforded in this reception a real participation in the resurrected Christ and an anticipatory taste of the Zionic "feast of rich food, a feast of well-aged wines, of rich food filled with marrow, of well-aged wines strained clear" (Isa. 25:6, Easter Evening).

After consuming this heavenly feast, Christians return to their seats in serene spiritual satiation, sitting next to the disciples as they share their final breakfast with Jesus. They experience a brief moment of quiet intimacy with Jesus just as the disciples experienced on the beach. But just as the disciples soon after witnessed Jesus depart from their eyes, Christians too must soon after their Eucharistic meal depart from the church. The time of the new creation is at hand, but its completion is still in the distance. And so the church must continue its journey to Mount Zion, learning to grow in their love and knowledge of Jesus Christ as they await his return. For this reason, the church year moves from Easter to Ordinary Time, the time of living in obedience to Christ in this present age.

CHAPTER 6

WIND *and* FIRE

Christ's Spirit for Us

Pentecost A, B, C, Easter 2A, 5A, 6A, 5C, 7C

Almighty God, on this day, through the outpouring of the Holy Spirit, you revealed the way of eternal life to every race and nation: Pour out this gift anew, that by the preaching of the Gospel your salvation may reach to the ends of the earth; through Jesus Christ our Lord, who lives and reigns with you, in the unity of the Holy Spirit, one God, for ever and ever. Amen.

Collect for Whitsunday (2019 BCP)

HOLY WEEK chronicles the ways in which Jesus enables forgiveness of sins through the cross and conquers the deadly effects of sin through his resurrection. The remainder of the Easter season details the ways in which human beings can receive this forgiveness and enter into the new creation of which Christ is the firstfruits. The lectionary readings for Easter thus focus on the sending of the Holy Spirit upon those who profess faith in the resurrected Christ, with the season culminating in the great outpouring of the Holy Spirit at Pentecost.

The sending of the Holy Spirit and the Spirit's empowerment of the disciples for mission to the ends of the earth are the most prominent themes throughout the Easter season. While the Easter season ends with Pentecost, the preceding weeks serve to unpack the ramifications of Pentecost on the life of the church. This comes principally through the chronicling of the mission of the disciples throughout the book of Acts, which is included in nearly every Sunday leading up to and including Pentecost.

The descent of the Holy Spirit at Pentecost is described through a number of symbols and actions, all of which aid in our understanding of the person and work of the Spirit. While all three years for Pentecost Day include Luke's portrayal of Pentecost (Acts 2:1–21) and a portion of Psalm 104, the lectionary includes different Old Testament and Epistle readings for each of these years. These passages are chosen in order to highlight one specific symbol present at Pentecost, and in turn to highlight one particular aspect of the Holy Spirit's movement in the world. Year B focuses on the symbol of wind and the Spirit as the agent of new creation. Year A focuses on the symbol of pouring in order to show how the Spirit equips all those who profess faith in Christ. Year C examines the symbol of fire to show how the

Spirit empowers Christians to proclaim the gospel to the ends of the earth.

Wind and Breath

Wind is invisible air in motion. We cannot see the wind, but we see the effects of the wind as it encounters physical entities. The movement of trees indicates the presence of storm winds, and an ocean breeze is experienced through the cooling effect it has on our skin. Wind is also generated in human bodies through the process of breathing. When we breathe and when we speak, we push wind out of our mouths and nostrils and into the environment around us.

As the invisible power and presence of God, the Holy Spirit is frequently manifested as wind and breath in order to show how God both creates and sustains life. The Holy Spirit's presence is shown in the presence of wind hovering over the waters at the beginning of the creation account in Genesis 1, and likewise the Spirit is depicted as the breath of God giving life to Adam in Genesis 2. While the Spirit is associated with the beginning of creation, it is likewise associated with the re-creation and renewal of life. As the Psalm selection for Pentecost shows, it is God who withdraws his breath of life for a humanity steeped in sin, yet it is this very same wind of the Spirit that has the potential to "renew the face of the earth" (Ps. 104:31).

The violent wind that rushes into the gathering of disciples at Pentecost indicates that this time of renewal and re-creation is at hand. In light of Jesus's victory over sin and death, and in light of his ascension to heaven, the breath of God can now be sent down like wind to fill the lungs of his followers with new life. The resurrected body of Jesus is the firstfruits of new creation, and in the reception of the Holy Spirit at Pentecost those gathered became partakers of these firstfruits. The specific date of this occurrence indicates the power of the Spirit to bring about new creation: Pentecost is the day reserved for the Jewish festival of firstfruits, and its occurrence—fifty days after the resurrection—symbolizes the Year of Jubilee, a period of rest and renewal.

As Pentecost shows, those who profess faith in Jesus Christ are enabled to be receptacles of the Holy Spirit, to have the very breath of God coursing through their lungs. The workings of the Spirit through Christians, a movement that began on this day, will continue until the Spirit is fully manifested through every inch of the earth. Christians living in the time after Pentecost and before the second coming of Christ thus live in a transition period, the "already-not-yet" time in which, as Paul says, the old creation is passing while the new creation is emerging. The Epistle reading from Romans for Pentecost B highlights this ever-present tension that marks Christians on their sojourn. According to Paul, Christians have received the firstfruits of the Spirit in their souls, yet they must endure the passing away of their old bodies as they await their own resurrection. As a result, Christians groan, along with the rest of creation, eagerly hoping for the completion of Christ's victory which began in his resurrection.

This final victory is described in the Old Testament reading for Pentecost B, where Ezekiel exhorts the breath of Jesus, the Spirit of God, to rush down on the valley of bones just as it rushed down on Pentecost (Ezek. 37:1–14). Just as the wind of the Spirit rushed through the waters at creation, just as it cascaded down the mountains to the disciples to inaugurate the new creation, it will rush through the valley to complete the process of renewal, knitting together the bones and sinews of the faithful departed.

Pouring

The rushing wind of the Spirit at Pentecost coursed through the lungs of every believing Christian assembled, no matter their socioeconomic status or place of origin. Peter sees in this gathering of Christians from around the world the fulfillment of the prophet Joel: "In the last days it will be, God declares, that I will pour out my Spirit upon all flesh, and your sons and your daughters shall prophesy" (Acts 2:17; Joel 2:28). Pentecost initiates these last days, which are marked by the pouring out of the Holy Spirit to *everyone* who calls upon the name of Jesus as Lord.

Pouring is the movement of liquid from one location to another. It often connotes lavishness and abundance, as in the pouring out of drinks for festive occasions. The pouring out of water and oil is used throughout the Old Testament to indicate the movement of the Holy Spirit. Oil is poured out on the heads of priests and kings to empower them with the Spirit. On Mount Eden, there is a continuous pouring out of water by means of the river of life. Here, water is able to descend from one place to another without the fountainhead drying up. The sin of Adam and Eve resulted in a hemming up of this water and a restriction of the Holy Spirit. The Old Testament selection for Pentecost A reveals this limited manifestation of the Spirit. Here, the Holy Spirit, which was bestowed on Moses, is momentarily poured out upon the assembled seventy elders, allowing them to briefly prophesy in the Spirit. Later, Eldad and Medad receive the Spirit and in turn prophesy, prompting Moses to yearn for the day when all of Israel would receive this Spirit, and all God's people prophesy (Num. 11:24–30).

An optional Epistle reading for Pentecost A (1 Cor. 12:3–13) shows that Moses's wish has come true through the great outpouring of the Holy Spirit at Pentecost. In this passage, Paul declares that the entire gathering of Christians in the church receive the same Spirit, and it is this one Spirit that gives a differentiation of gifts to all Christians, gifts that are in turn meant to build up the unity of the church. For Paul, Christians have received the same Spirit as Moses, and this Spirit is opulently poured out on all just as it was poured out on Eldad and Medad. The reception of this Spirit is not, however, poured out indiscriminately: It is still only on those who profess faith in Jesus Christ. As Jesus states in the Gospel reading for Pentecost A (John 7:37–39), it is only out of the *believer's* heart that will flow streams of living water, but this water is offered to everyone who professes this belief.

Fire

The other great symbol of Pentecost is fire. Like wind, fire is immaterial yet powerful. Though it cannot be grasped by human hands, it is capable of illuminating large buildings and leveling entire cities. Fire retains its same unique properties even as it grows and spreads throughout vast terrains.

The lectionary readings for Pentecost C highlight the Spirit as the fiery presence of God, destroying the enemies of God yet empowering the faithful for the mission of God. They do this by foregrounding the account of the building and destruction of the tower of Babel in Genesis 11. In this passage, humanity unites to build a skyscraper tall enough to challenge God in the heavens. To reach these heights, they harness the power of fire to make bricks and force slaves to build their monstrosity. However, God brings down his own fire to destroy the tower, scattering humankind to the ends of the earth. The lectionary pairs this passage with the Pentecost story in order to show how Acts serves as a reversal of Genesis 11. At Babel, humankind unites to challenge God by leveraging fire. At Pentecost, the disciples gather together to wait on the fire from above. At Babel, God's fire destroys the tower, while on Pentecost, the fire of the Holy Spirit rests as tongues on every believer, yet none are destroyed.

The rest of the readings for Pentecost C tease out the implications of the fire of the Spirit's descent on the church. In the lection from Romans, Paul states that those who receive the Spirit have a kind of childlike intimacy with God, an intimacy that permits them to call him Father. The domineering might of Babel is contrasted with the childlike intimacy of Pentecost. Jesus reiterates this point in the Gospel lection, telling his disciples that those who receive the Spirit have received the light of truth and are now capable of following his commandments. In addition, Jesus declares that his disciples will be empowered to do even greater works than himself. The fire of the Spirit will enable his followers to carry on his ministry with even greater scope.

The remainder of the book of Acts showcases these great and powerful works of the disciples as they proclaim the resurrected Christ to the ends of the earth. Just as Babel led to the scattering of nations through a destructive fire, the fire of the Spirit empowers the disciples to journey to these nations to gather God's people and unite them with the Spirit. The lectionary readings throughout the Easter season draw from Acts to beautifully highlight how the Spirit empowers the disciples to proclaim the gospel like wildfire to an expanding number of persons and territories. The Spirit empowers Peter and Stephen to preach to the Israelites (2A, 5A), then the Spirit opens a door to the Gentiles through the vision of Peter (5C) and the ministry of Paul (7C), which we see evidenced in Paul's great speech at the Areopagus (6A).

Wind and Fire in the Church Today

The Holy Spirit is continuously at work in the worship, ministry, and mission of the church. Within the Eucharistic assembly, the Spirit is most vividly seen in the epiclesis: The invocation of the Holy Spirit by the priest upon the bread and wine. Here the assembly experiences a kind of mini-Pentecost: The bread on the table is produced through the gathering of wheat and fire; it is "pure bread that is made with fire and sanctified with invocations."[1] Just as the fire of the Spirit empowered the disciples to proclaim the gospel and gather Christians from all nations, the bread gathers together seed and binds it together with fire. The pastor then breathes over the bread and wine, asking God to send his "Holy Spirit upon these gifts that they may be the Sacrament of the Body of Christ and his Blood of the new Covenant."[2] Then they pray that the Spirit would unite the church just as the bread is united in a single loaf: "Unite us to your Son in his sacrifice." Just as the Spirit rushes through at Pentecost, the Spirit moves through the breath of the pastor's words, enabling the bread and wine to become food of the new creation. In receiving this bread, the church experiences a unity not unlike that experienced at Pentecost.

The outpouring of the Holy Spirit at Pentecost is a stream that continues to flow down to all believers to this day. Each and every Christian, no matter their age or ability, is given the same Spirit and is bestowed gifts meant for the building up of the church. Clergy and laity alike are all given some distinct gift by virtue of their baptism. And all are called to bring forth their gifts for the building up of the body of Christ. These gifts are made manifest in the life of the local congregation by the participation of the laity in the various roles and responsibilities of both Christian worship and Christian life. Laypersons lead prayers, read Scripture, facilitate congregational singing, and, in many contexts, preach. The bulletins at church and the announcements during the service highlight the "bountiful distribution of the Spirit" manifested in various ministries and missions spearheaded by the diverse gifts of the church's members.[3]

It is one of the chief responsibilities of the minister to continuously hand over authority to all members of the church. The minister is called to further pour out the Spirit on all in the congregation, searching for ways for every member to vitally contribute to the worship and ministry of the church. Clergy err when they refuse to hand over ministry, preventing the Eldads and Medads in their midst from flourishing. In so doing, they strip Christians of their spiritual birthright, turning the church into a mere event produced by a special class of trained clerical professionals rather than the body of Christ. Such failures, however, can also occur through the neglect of laypersons to accept their spiritual authority when they refuse opportunities to volunteer in the various aspects of church life. The megachurch where thousands of people gather to see one pastor and five musicians on a stage and the small church with an overworked pastor who does everything from preach to mow the lawn both have in common this failure of all the saints to fully participate in the life of the church.

Finally, the church continues to spread the fire of the Holy Spirit through the active proclamation of the gospel to those who are not Christian. By virtue of their baptism and confession of faith, every member of the church receives a tongue of fire, and every Christian is called from time to time to proclaim the gospel alongside Peter and Paul. Sunday worship is a chance to have this fire kindled in the hearts of every Christian, with the hopes that every person in the church will spread the fire of the Spirit through active engagement with their unbelieving acquaintances. Like the fiery mission of Peter and Paul, such engagement should involve the verbal declaration of Christ's death and resurrection and an explicit invitation for their interlocutors to believe in Jesus as Lord and God. Christians should take their cues from Peter, Paul, and Stephen as shown throughout the lectionary readings. They should seek to be persuasive in their interactions, marshaling forth a variety of arguments for the truth of the Christian faith and modeling this truth in acts of love and healing. Yet such persuasive acts must also be bold and uncompromising. The Christian may have to endure awkward or uncomfortable conversations and may have to risk a friendship as they reveal the ways that Christianity clashes with modern morals and dogmas.

Over time, this active proclamation of the gospel will manifest itself in a diverse body of Christians who gather together each week for church. This body will be comprised not just of lifelong Christians or Christians who have simply migrated from one church to another, but it will also include a substantial number of converts who have come to faith in part through the labors of existing members. These new believers are knitted together through the Holy Spirit as they gather together as the body of Christ. And just as the lectionary chronicles the empowering work of the Spirit throughout Easter, it also documents the power of this Spirit to knit together the church in communion.

CHAPTER 7

COMMUNION

Christ's Body Broken for Us

Maundy Thursday, Easter 3A, 4A, 5A, 3C, Proper 12B, 13B

Almighty and everlasting God, by whose Spirit the whole body of the Church is governed and sanctified: hear our prayer which we offer for all your faithful people, that in their vocation and ministry they may serve you in holiness and truth to the glory of your name; through our Lord and Saviour Jesus Christ, who is alive and reigns with you, in the unity of the Holy Spirit, one God, now and for ever.

Fifth Sunday of Ordinary Time (Book of Common Worship, Church of England)

THE EASTER SEASON details the sending of the Spirit and the empowerment of the disciples to proclaim the gospel to the ends of the earth.

But the lectionary readings for this season also describe what happens *after* the success of these acts of the apostles, which involves the formation of new gatherings centered upon the worship of God the Father, Son, and Holy Spirit, and a common life grounded in the love of Christ. The readings for Easter season and beyond chronicle the formation of the first of these church communities and unpack their nature and function through the symbols of stone and bread.

Stones

Stones are hard and ubiquitous. They are found in nearly all environments and are capable of supporting a massive amount of weight from natural and man-made material. As such, the symbol of the stone is synonymous with foundations: the ground on which sturdy structures are built.

We have already seen the stone introduced as a key symbol on Holy Saturday and Easter Sunday. The stone that seals the tomb of Joseph of Arimathea indicates the real and complete bodily death of Jesus, yet this same stone rolled away indicates the real and complete resurrection of Jesus. The stone is thus a symbol of the resurrection as historical fact and ground of the Christian faith. As the grounding of the Christian faith, the resurrection is also the foundational stone of the community formed out of believers who profess this faith. The reference to Jesus Christ as the cornerstone is a common symbol threaded throughout the Easter season: Peter identifies Jesus as the "stone that the builders rejected" (Easter 4B), while the psalmist declares that Jesus is his "strong rock, a castle to keep [him] safe" (Easter 5A).

In describing Jesus as the chief cornerstone, the foundational stone of a castle, Scripture is intentionally inviting readers to compare this cornerstone to the stones of the temple in Jerusalem. A massive structure built by human hands, the temple was the fixed place set aside for the worship of God, and the only place where priests could perform the ritual sacrifices necessary to provide a temporary reprieve from the guilt of sin. But on Good Friday, Jesus provides a final sacrifice for sin, tearing the temple curtain in two and permanently abolishing the need for the ongoing animal sacrifices facilitated by the Jerusalem temple.

Good Friday destroys the spiritual necessity of the temple, and the effects of this event would play themselves out in history with the physical destruction of the temple during the age of the apostles. But in destroying the need for a fixed temple, Jesus did not abolish the need for the people of God to continue to worship and sacrifice. Instead, worship is now grounded upon the resurrected Christ as cornerstone. The lectionary readings for the Easter season, particularly the readings from 5A, show how this symbol of the stone extends to the entire gathering of Christians in the church. In Peter's first epistle, he reiterates that Jesus is the living stone who was rejected by humans yet chosen by God. Then, he states something remarkable: that followers of Christ are *also* living stones, meant to form a spiritual house of worship. The stones of the physical temple in Jerusalem no longer demarcate the space by which the true worship of God will take place. Instead, the temple is reconstituted by Christians *each and every time* they gather together to worship Jesus Christ. This has two implications for the life of Christians, both of which are teased out in the lectionary readings.

First, since the stones of the temple are now living beings, worship can take place wherever Christians gather. The true temple is essentially built every Sunday when the living stones of baptized Christians gather together in one place. This means that full and true worship of God is no longer restricted to one particular physical structure or one particular locale. The lectionary readings for the Easter season chronicle the establishment of multiple churches in places far away from Jerusalem. The first reading from 5A draws out this connection through the death of Stephen. Stephen's speech in Jerusalem leads the onlookers to cast him out of the city and kill him with stones. The stones hurled at Stephen represent the rejection of many Israelites of their invitation to become the living stones of the church. But these stones also demarcate the beginning of the expansion of the living stones of God's people to the ends of the earth. Saul, standing at the foot of Stephen's stoned body, is affected by the sight and will soon convert to Christianity and carry on this mission to create living stones throughout the gentile world.

Second, the characterization of Christians as the living stones of the spiritual temple implies the necessity for all Christians to gather for worship and the fundamental equality of all Christians within the church. According to Scripture, there is but one cornerstone: Christ crucified and risen. There is no hierarchy of importance in regard to the remaining "living stones," and all are required to attend worship so as to build the spiritual temple. A church whose members refuse to gather is like a temple whose stones are missing. Peter's epistle from 5A draws out this implication of Christians as living stones by immediately declaring that each Christian is also part of a royal priesthood, offering "spiritual sacrifices acceptable to God through Jesus Christ" (1 Pet. 2:5). Just as there is no hierarchy of living stones, there are no castes in the spiritual temple; all are priests, as vital and important for the worship of God as the individual priests of the Old Testament temple. But this fundamental equality bears with it a great responsibility. If all are priests, all are required to offer sacrifices, just as the Old Testament priests were required to offer temple sacrifices. These are, according to Peter, "spiritual sacrifices," in which Christians offer up their hearts, their time, and their energy in the worship of Christ in his church and in the proclamation of his resurrection to those outside of the church.

Bread

While the symbol of stone speaks to the universality of the church and the equality of its members, the symbol of bread speaks to the quality of life within these gatherings of living stones. The lectionary readings from the Easter season, as well as several weeks from Ordinary Time, feature the symbol of bread as part of numerous miracles performed by Jesus. In addition, the Easter season passages drawn from the book of Acts depict the quality of the first churches, who physically manifest the communion that bread symbolizes.

Bread is a sign of life. As the most basic of staples, bread is synonymous in many cultures with food itself. Like other foods, bread is made through a kind of death: Plants must be destroyed and harvested for their grain, which is then gathered together and pounded to make flour. And when this bread is baked and consumed, it provides life and sustenance to those who eat it. In eating bread, we implicitly acknowledge that something had to die for us to live.

On Maundy Thursday, Jesus pronounced that the bread he held was his body, broken for his disciples, and gave instructions to the church to continue to pronounce this blessing and receive bread as his body whenever they gather as living stones. In the specific act of breaking the bread, Christians are reminded that Jesus was broken, that his life was expelled so that they might receive the very life of God. In eating this bread, they in turn receive the very life of Jesus. The appearance of Jesus on the road to Emmaus, included in Easter 3A, makes this point even further. Even though Jesus unpacks the entirety of the Scriptures to Cleopas and the other disciple, this teaching is not enough for them to recognize him as risen Lord. It is only when Jesus breaks bread that they see him with the spiritual eyes of faith. At that moment, Jesus vanishes before their eyes. They see within this breaking of the bread the very mystery of faith: Christ has died, Christ is risen, Christ will come again. In eating this bread, they receive the very life of Christ as they await his return.

This symbol of bread is further developed in the season of Ordinary Time through a series of teachings that Jesus gives after the miracle of the multiplication of the loaves. Proper 12B pairs together the miracle of the multiplication of the loaves performed by both Elisha and Jesus. Both of these passages indicate the abundant nature of life with Jesus through the *excess* of bread produced. All those who partook of this spiritual bread ate until they were full, an anticipatory encounter of the heavenly feast of Mount Zion. Proper 13B continues with John's account of this miracle, in which Jesus declares to the onlookers that he is the Bread of Life, and that those who receive him will never go hungry. This passage is paired in the lectionary with Exodus 16 and Psalm 78, which describe the manna in the desert as the bread of heaven and the bread of angels. These passages are collated together in order to show that the ongoing reception of communion by Christians is at that same time a reception of the body of Christ and the bread of heaven.

Bread is also a symbol of fellowship. Just as eating bread provides life, the sharing of bread is a literal sharing in life. Throughout every civilization, meals are one of the primary ways that individuals draw close to one another. Meals both establish intimacy between friends and are a manifestation of intimacy between friends. The ongoing sharing of meals can create a kind of virtuous cycle of fellowship: People who eat together will draw close to one another, and in turn *will want* to eat together more often.

In Scripture, the breaking of bread is associated with a communal meal with God, and it is within the context of a meal that Jesus's glory is revealed to his disciples. In addition to Maundy Thursday and the miracle of the loaves, the lectionary highlights one of the last acts of Jesus before his resurrection (John 21:1–19, Easter 3C): Jesus allows for a miraculous catch of fish and prepares a meal of fish and bread for his disciples. It is within the intimacy of this breakfast meal that Jesus restores and commissions Peter to "feed his sheep," in so doing exhorting Peter to continue to nourish the followers of Jesus through the ongoing breaking of bread.

The word used to describe the community that is knit together through this shared meal with Jesus is *communion*, a complex word that shares an etymology with *common*, *community*, *union*, and *communication*. It is "the union of persons to God and each other through the power of the Holy Spirit, which enables such unity to be instantiated as the body of Christ."[1] Hence the lectionary leads the church from the sending of the Holy Spirit at Pentecost to the instantiation of the first gatherings of the body of Christ. In depicting these churches that emerge through the mission of the apostles, the book of Acts (Acts 2, Easter 4A) describes a gathering of people who devoted themselves to the apostles' teaching and to "the breaking of bread." The union with God and each other experienced in these gatherings led these early Christians to be overwhelmed with joy, and this joy prompted them to share their possessions in common and give to those in need.

This description of a common life in Acts 2 remains foreign to our contemporary understanding of the church. We live in a society that emphasizes the accumulation of possessions in order to increase economic utility, with the sharing of goods being restricted primarily to the family household. The household of the church, however, is supposed to extend to all those who participate in the Eucharistic meal. We are invited through the breaking of bread to cultivate the kinds of intimacy with those in the church that we typically have only with family, with the natural result that we seek to continually bless others with the possessions we have.

Stones and Bread in the Church Today

As the season of Easter shows, the mission of the apostles to proclaim the resurrected Christ did not end when their interlocutors believed in Jesus as Lord and God. Instead, conversion led to baptism and the immediate incorporation of the newly baptized into the common life of the church. Each Christian became a living stone of the spiritual temple at the moment of their baptism, and today Christians are likewise called to live into their birthright through *attendance* and *participation* in weekly worship.

First and foremost, Christians live into their calling as living stones through their attendance at worship services each week. Attendance is necessary—we see no indication at all in Scripture of the *option* to attend worship. A church whose members rarely attend is as deficient as a building with missing stones and gaping holes. Once one turns attendance into an option, one to be weighed against the desire to rest, travel, work, and play sports, they have already failed to take seriously their calling to be living stones knit together in the church.

Christians express their full equality in the life of the church by participating in all aspects of the worship service. Unlike in the Old Testament temple, there is nothing done in secret by a priest behind a veil. Everything is performed together by both clergy and laity alike. Even in some traditions that restrict the celebration of the Eucharist to ordained priests and presbyters, such authority is only exercised with the participation and consent of the gathered congregation. The Eucharist is a shared meal that requires shared participants. All baptized Christians are, in the words of Nicholas Afanasiev, priests who "concelebrate" the Eucharist together with the clergy.[2] This is evidenced in the required responses of the congregation throughout the communion service, responses which culminate in the great communal "amen" declared after the invocation of the Holy Spirit upon the bread and wine.

The worship service as a whole reaches its zenith shortly after this great "amen," when the bread is visibly fractured and consumed by the living stones gathered. In the breaking of the bread, the church is taken up into sacred time, reliving the moment when Jesus broke bread on the road to Emmaus. In the breaking, they see with the spiritual eyes of faith that Jesus is present. When they receive and eat this bread, the divine life of Jesus is given over to them. His life for their life. The bread that is gathered from many stalks of wheat becomes the divine bread of

God that gathers together Christians, knitting them in the love of God and in communion fellowship around Jesus Christ. The words that are spoken upon the reception of the bread reveal it to be at once the heavenly manna from above and the very body of Jesus: On any given Sunday, one might hear either "the bread of heaven" or "the body of Christ" as they receive.

Churches whose members attend regularly and receive the Eucharist will see signs of communion sprouting up in their midst. Members will cultivate relationships with each other outside of Sunday gatherings and will begin offering up their homes and their resources for the building up of each other. These signs of communion will in turn contribute to a virtuous cycle, fostering in Christians an increased excitement to gather together again each Sunday. Attendance, participation, and reception of shared bread often do more than any sermon or program to build this awe-inspiring fellowship.

CHAPTER 8

FAITH

Christ Our Living Water

Easter Vigil, Epiphany 1 (All Years), Lent 2A, 2B, 2C, Easter 2A, B, C, Easter 3C

Almighty and everlasting Father, in your great mercy you saved Noah and his family in the Ark from the destruction of the flood, prefiguring the Sacrament of Holy Baptism. Look mercifully upon these your servants. Wash and sanctify them through your Holy Spirit, that they may be delivered from destruction and received into the Ark of Christ's Church; and being steadfast in faith, joyful through hope, and rooted in love, they may pass through the turbulent floods of this troublesome world and come into the land of everlasting life, through Jesus Christ our Lord. Amen.

Prayer for Baptismal Candidates (2019 BCP)

THE LECTIONARY walks Christians through the life, death, resurrection, and ascension of Jesus Christ. It chronicles the ways that Jesus fulfills the entirety of the Old Testament promises, provides true forgiveness of sin, and enables both Jew and gentile alike to return to God. The barrier preventing humanity from returning to the mountain of God's presence has been lifted; what remains is for individuals to decide if they wish to return to God by believing in his Son, Jesus Christ. A profession of faith in Jesus Christ as Lord and God, sealed in the waters of baptism, is what is required of individuals to make this return. In so doing, they acknowledge the objective reality of Jesus as God and Lord and make this objective reality subjective in their own lives.

The lectionary provides ample opportunities for individuals to profess their faith and affirm it in the waters of Christian baptism. Faith and baptism are perhaps the most pervasive themes in the lectionary: Advent is highlighted by John's ministry of baptism, the first Sunday of Epiphany celebrates the baptism of Jesus, the faith of Abraham is a key component of Lent, and the faith of Thomas is celebrated on the first Sunday of Easter in all three years.

The lectionary sprinkles these passages throughout the Christian year for two reasons. First, so that seekers may be presented with frequent invitations to believe in Jesus Christ as Lord and Savior. The lectionary is, contrary to popular opinion, very seeker-sensitive: Every four to six weeks involves a passage exhorting newcomers to profess faith in Christ and to seal this faith in the waters of baptism. Second, the lectionary includes frequent baptismal passages so that Christians may make a habit of constantly professing their faith and reaffirming their baptismal vows. Faith itself is strengthened in these frequent professions. A marriage begins with a vow of love and fidelity, and these vows are strengthened and affirmed through the continuous uttering of "I love you" each day. In many ways, married couples spend their whole lives learning to discover the meaning of the vows they took on their wedding day. Likewise, the vows of faith declared at baptism are strengthened by frequent invitations to affirm Christian belief, and the Christian life is a journey whereby we learn more and more about the faith we declare. Through the various seasons of the church calendar, the lectionary seeks to unfold the content of Christian faith through an examination of individual professions of faith and through the symbol of water.

Faith in Key Biblical Figures

The lectionary elucidates the Christian faith through the lives of two key figures: Abraham and Thomas. Through Abraham the church learns the quality of Christian faith, and through Thomas the church learns the content of its faith.

The second week of Lent for all years includes an Old Testament selection from the story of Abraham, coupled (in Lent 2A and 2B) with Paul's exposition of the life of Abraham from the book of Romans. Abraham is the embodiment of faith in the Old Testament, and it is through

Abraham that we learn the key attributes of faith. The selections from Lent 2A highlight the simplicity of faith: Abraham is called by God to leave behind country and livelihood, and he obeys without question (Gen. 12:1–4). God provides no rationale for this calling, and Abraham provides no resistance. Paul expands upon this simple act of obedience in the selection from Romans for this Sunday (4:1–5), declaring that Abraham was considered righteous in this simple act of faith *before* he accomplished his mighty works. Paul then uses this reflection on Abraham as a springboard to show how righteousness cannot be obtained by following the law (vv. 13–17). Lent 2A pairs these readings with the conversation of Jesus and Nicodemus (John 3:1–17), which highlights the necessity of salvation from above and not through the works of the flesh. When read together, these lections paint a picture of faith as simple, trusting, and unwavering obedience to the will of God. For Abraham, this simple faith led to a greater understanding of God and an abundance of great works, but these things flowed out of his initial act of trust, rather than leading to it.

The Old Testament readings for Lent 2B and 2C chronicle the promises given to Abraham from God: the promise of abundant descendants (Gen. 17:1–7, 15–16, 2B) and a land for God's people (Gen. 15:1–12, 17–18, 2C). When Abraham asks for assurances of these promises, he is invited to perform a ritual sacrifice of animals, binding himself to God in a covenant. Abraham here models another central quality of faith: trust in things unseen. God's promise that Abraham's descendants will number like the stars is striking in that it requires Abraham to believe that which is impossible by nature—that he will bear a son by a barren woman. In addition, it is a promise that can only be fulfilled long after he has died.

The Epistle readings for 2B and 2C show how the Christian faith is likewise a trust in things unseen, things that cannot be proven, and things that will come to pass only after our deaths. For Paul (Rom. 4:13–25, 2B), the unwavering trust of Abraham in the promises of God was meant to inspire Christians to place their unwavering trust in the resurrection of Christ and, through it, the justification of sinners. In his letter to the Philippians (Phil. 3:17–4:1, 2C), Paul likewise implores Christians to trust in the resurrection of their own bodies in the midst of a decaying world. Just as Abraham had to trust that God would keep his promises long after his death, Christians in turn trust that God will bring about their own resurrection long after their present lives expire. As Abraham gained assurance of these promises through ritual sacrifice, Christians likewise receive assurances in the once-for-all sacrifice of Jesus Christ, which is celebrated each Sunday through bread and wine.

While the lectionary readings for the second week of Lent describe the quality of faith, the readings for the second week of Easter tell us of the content of Christian faith, which is Jesus Christ's death and resurrection. Each of these weeks includes the same Gospel passage: the story of Thomas's doubt and his declaration that Jesus is Lord and God (John 20:19–31). Each week then pairs this Gospel reading with at least one other selection that invites faith in Jesus Christ through the witness of his resurrection. Easter 2A (Acts 2:14, 22–32) features Peter's great post-Pentecost sermon, in which he implores his audience to believe in Jesus, whom "God raised up, and of that all of us are witnesses" (v. 32). Easter 2C (Acts 5:27–32) likewise includes Peter witnessing to Christ and inviting repentance. The Epistle reading for 2A (1 Pet. 1:3–9) connects the reality of faith in the resurrection to the new birth that comes in baptism. Easter 2B (1 John 1:1–2:2) includes John's testimony of his own faith sparked by a physical encounter with the resurrected Christ.

All these passages for the second week of Easter culminate in the encounter of Thomas with the resurrected Christ. Thomas is the stand-in for the individual hearer of John's Gospel. Nonbelievers begin as skeptics, hearing the story of the resurrection but wanting more evidence. But through a personal encounter with Christ, they are given the opportunity to utter the words of Thomas, the simplest expression of the Christian faith: "My Lord and my God." Here in this statement lie the core commitments of Christianity: that Jesus is God and that Christians must commit themselves to following him as Lord. The major difference, however, between Thomas and contemporary Christians is that Thomas physically saw and touched the resurrected Christ—thus Jesus says in front of the believing Thomas, "Blessed are those who believe but do not see" (John 20:29). Thomas's faith begins with a physical encounter with Jesus Christ that leads him to affirm the spiritual reality that this carpenter from Nazareth is God incarnate. Faith comes today through a spiritual encounter with Jesus as Lord and God, materially sealed in the waters of baptism, and culminating in a physical vision of Jesus on Mount Zion. For Thomas, sight culminates in belief; for us, belief culminates in sight.

Salvation Through Water

Water and rescue. Water is a symbol of chaos and destruction. Those surprised at sea by a sudden storm are often overcome by sheer terror and helplessness at the overpowering waves. Despite the great technological advancements of the modern world, whole cities can still be leveled by a devastating flood. And even the calmest of waters can prove deadly for those unable to swim. In Scripture, water is often associated with the chaotic nature of sin. Like a raging storm, sin brings unpredictability, devastation, and ultimately death. To escape these turbulent waters, one must turn to God, who alone is able to rescue us from sin and death.

Throughout the church year, the lectionary highlights the ability of God to rescue humanity from the chaotic waters through baptism in Jesus Christ. The readings for the first week of Epiphany draw out the connection between God's ability to physically and spiritually tame the turbulent waters. The Old Testament selection for 1B, Genesis 1:1–5, shows how the creation of the world was brought about in part through the Holy Spirit sweeping over turbulent waters, and the Psalm selection, Psalm 29, affirms that the "voice of God is upon the waters," and as a result the waters are in his control (v. 3). The Old

Testament selections for Epiphany 1C and 1A show how this power of God to physically control the waters is the same power that can spiritually rescue those caught in the chaotic waters of sin. In Isaiah 43:1–7 (1C), God assures his people that he will rescue them safely through troubled waters of life, a rescue performed by God's servant whom the Spirit uniquely rests upon (Isa. 42:1–9, 1A).

These readings for the first week of Epiphany culminate in the Gospel accounts of the baptism of Jesus (Matt. 3:13–17; Mark 1:4–11; Luke 3:15–17, 21–22). Jesus is the Christ, the one anointed with the Spirit to bring about the rescue of humanity. The presence of the Holy Spirit in the form of a dove and the voice of the Father draw together these Old Testament lections: The voice of God, the voice that is upon the waters, is the very same voice of Jesus. And the Spirit that hovered over the waters at creation is the same Spirit that rests upon Jesus. In passing through the waters of the Jordan, Jesus reveals that he is the one appointed to take humankind through the chaotic waters of sin and death. In so doing, he sanctifies water, enabling it to be the vessel through which salvation is sealed in the hearts of all who profess faith in him as Lord and God. He "imparted of the fragrance of His Godhead to the waters,"[1] mixing the Spirit with water and enabling Christians to partake in the Holy Spirit through their own baptism.

The fulfillment of water as the vessel through which humanity is rescued is most explicit in the lectionary readings for Lent 1B. Here, Mark's account of Jesus's baptism (Mark 1:9–15) is paired with the rescue of Noah and his family from the great flood (Gen. 9:8–17). God gives Noah a rainbow as a sign, with the promise that "never again shall all flesh be cut off by the waters of a flood, and never again shall there be a flood to destroy the earth" (v. 11). The Epistle selection from 1 Peter ties these two passages together, explicitly stating that the flood prefigures Christian baptism (3:18–22). The joining of these passages invites Christians to see their baptism as a type of Noahic rescue from death: Just as Noah was saved from physical death on the wood of the ark, Christians are saved from eternal death by crossing the waters of baptism on the wood of the cross. The permanency of God's declaration to Noah is pronounced on those who cross the waters of baptism. They are granted assurance of their rescue from death and have no need of further baptisms.

Water and cleansing. Peter's great description of baptism as a type of Noahic rescue from death ends by asserting that baptism rescues not by cleaning dirt from the body, but by a cleansing of conscience (1 Pet. 3:21). This introduces a second major understanding of baptism through the symbol of water: a cleansing of sin.

The cleansing power of water is obvious to anyone who has been dirty. We bathe with water to remove dirt and smells, often applying oils and lotions to the skin after the process. We wash our hands before meals not only to clean them but also to prevent dirt from contaminating food. Throughout the Bible, this cleansing of dirt with water is correlated liturgically to the cleansing of sin from the soul. The presence of lavers in the tabernacle and temple indicated a continual need to be cleansed of sin before partaking in ritual sacrifice. John the Baptist's ministry of baptism was centered particularly on a baptism of repentance, a physical act meant to indicate a spiritual desire to have one's sins forgiven.

The readings for Lent 1A focus on how Jesus's baptism allows Christian baptism to bring about permanent, lasting forgiveness of sin. They begin by recounting the first sins of Adam and Eve (Gen. 2:15–17; 3:1–7). The selection from Genesis 3 focuses on the unclean conscience of Adam and Eve, who neurotically cover themselves with the stuff of the earth in order to protect their nakedness. Genesis 3 will conclude with Adam and Eve's banishment: The waters of chaos will separate them from Eden forever. Their life is marked by an uncleanliness that matches the dirtiness of their souls; they toil among the dirt and don animal skins for protection.

In the Epistle selection from Lent 1A, Paul shows how Adam's sin was passed on to his descendants (Rom. 5:12–19). Though human beings may sin in different ways and in different proportion, all have inherited sin, and all will die as Adam died as a result of sin. But as the new Adam, Jesus is the complete, perfect, and obedient human being. The selections are thus paired with the account of Jesus's baptism (Matt. 4:1–11) to show that those who are baptized in Christ share in Jesus's obedience and righteousness. They are cleansed of their sins, leaving behind the old Adam to become children of the new Adam.

Life through water. Through his baptism in the River Jordan, Jesus calmed the raging waters, sanctifying them so that they might be a source of new birth and new life for all those who believe in him. Life is perhaps the most prominent mark of the symbol of water. Water is essential to human life, and the human body itself is composed primarily of water. Water flows in and out of the human body as part of its intertwining with the ecosystem. On Mount Eden, Adam and Eve were part of an ecosystem predicated upon the river of life—the formation of this river immediately precedes the creation of Adam. As such, their bodies were composed of water from this stream: The river of life coursed through their veins. As sin cut off access to Eden, it also prevented humankind from accessing this living water.

As we have seen, Jesus has made it possible for the Holy Spirit to infuse ordinary water so that it might bring about new life. In Christian baptism, the water becomes a temporary manifestation of the river of life, and those plunged in its waters can now have the river of life coursing through their veins once again. For this reason, baptism is referred to as a new birth, the "womb water" through which individuals are born of the Spirit.

The lectionary draws out passages from Scripture that highlight water as this basic symbol of birth and life. Lent 2A pairs the aforementioned passages concerning the faith of Abraham from Genesis and Romans with Jesus's conversation with Nicodemus in John 3, in which Jesus declares that one must be born from above, in a birth of water and Spirit. The recitation of these passages together is meant to show the connection between faith, baptism, and new life in Christ. Those who profess faith in Jesus Christ and pass through the waters of baptism are born from above by the Spirit. Just as a baby passes through amniotic waters in birth, Christians pass through living waters as they are born of the Spirit in baptism.

Those who are born from above continue to have the Spirit-filled waters of the river of life flowing through them throughout their existence. Lent 3A's passages are assembled to show how water is a symbol of the ongoing work of the Spirit in the life of the Christian. In the Gospel passage (John 4:5–42), Jesus declares to the woman at the well that those who believe in him will have "streams of living water" (i.e., the river of life) flowing through their bellies. The rest of the lectionary passages exhort Christians to remain confident that the God who poured out this water in baptism will continue to pour his Spirit into the hearts of the faithful. Romans 5:1–11 encourages Christians to cultivate the virtue of hope through suffering, which is made possible through the assurance that the love of God has been poured out, and continues to be poured out, to those who have received living water. Exodus 17:1–7 and Psalm 95 stand as warnings to Christians not to doubt in the midst of trials, as the Israelites doubted God in the wilderness. In the passage from Exodus, God makes water flow from a rock in order to show Israel that his ability to control water continues even after their baptism in the Red Sea. Christians in turn should not complain in the midst of their own wilderness-like trials, trusting instead that God will continue to pour out the living water of his Spirit even in the toughest of times.

Water and the Church Today

The lectionary invites those interested in Christianity to publicly declare their faith in Jesus as Lord and God and cement this faith through the waters of baptism. Its frequent incorporation of baptismal texts throughout the church year is meant to both invite faith and remind Christians to continually confirm and affirm their baptismal vows.

The church enacts these readings principally by initiating new members through the rite of baptism. In baptism, the candidates are invited to enter the salvific history of God's people, and the rite of baptism is designed to show how candidates both recapitulate and participate in the story of Scripture. The rite begins with a public declaration of consent, followed by a public rejection of Satan and all his works. Then, candidates publicly declare their full faith in Jesus as Lord by reciting the Apostles' Creed. The water is then consecrated by the pastor, enabling it to become the river of life for those who are plunged in its waters. In the threefold immersion in the name of the Father, Son, and Holy Spirit, the candidate joins in the baptism of Jesus, coming out of the waters to hear the voice of the Father and experience a manifestation of the Spirit. Those who take this plunge live out the words of Paul in Romans 6:3–5: They are united to Jesus's baptism, and to his death and resurrection. Finally, the candidate is sealed with the oil of the Holy Spirit. Now that they have crossed over the waters and back to God's presence, they receive the oil of the Tree of Life. They are "made partakers of the good olive-tree, Jesus Christ."[2]

The participatory aspect of baptism is most vividly seen when the rite is performed during the Easter Vigil service. Since Easter Vigil is the traditional service during which new believers are baptized, the primary thrust of the lectionary readings centers on the individual reception of baptism as participation in Jesus's baptism. Water is the key symbol threaded throughout a majority of the Easter Vigil readings. The readings begin with God taming the chaotic waters in Genesis 1 and continue with the account of the flood in Genesis 7. The presence of the dove and olive leaf at the end of the flood symbolizes the descent of the Holy Spirit, which comes when olive oil is poured out on the baptismal candidates. A detailed account of Israel's exodus (drawn from Exodus 14 and 15) chronicles the parting of the waters of the Red Sea and the demise of the Egyptian army once the Israelites had safely crossed. The destruction of this army indicates the destruction of evil demons accomplished through Jesus Christ and the sharing of this victory with all who are baptized. When the rite of baptism is performed after these readings, candidates can vividly see how their immersion in water is an immersion into the entire drama of salvation.

The rite of baptism is not only an opportunity for individuals to seal their faith in Christ, it is also an opportunity for baptized Christians to reaffirm their own faith. The recitation of the Apostles' Creed with the entire congregation is a moment to bolster one's own baptismal vows, akin to a married couple strengthening their vows through frequent compliments. A similar opportunity is given each week with the recitation of the Apostles' or

Nicene Creed. For those baptized as infants, confirmation is a moment to publicly declare the faith of their parents and to receive afresh the oil of the Spirit. Similar rites for reaffirmation and reception allow those whose faith has wavered, and those who have relocated, a chance to publicly recommit their faith.

Finally, the presence of water lavers at the entrance to the church affords an opportunity for weekly baptismal remembrance. As we dip our hands in these waters, we participate in the ceremonial washings in the tabernacle. In passing through these waters and into the sanctuary, we pass through the Red Sea and enter, for a time, onto the mountain of God, ready for heaven and earth to be briefly joined together as we worship God the Father, Son, and Holy Spirit.

Baptism initiates a lifelong journey. As the Israelites journeyed to Mount Sinai after crossing the Red Sea, Christians journey to Mount Zion with Jesus after crossing the waters of baptism. This pilgrimage is principally marked by obedience to Christ and a continual healing by Christ. The lectionary uses the season of Easter and Ordinary Time to chronicle this journey.

CHAPTER 9

OBEDIENCE

Christ Our Shepherd

Easter 4 A, B, C, Proper 10A, 11A, 12A, All Saints' Day A, B, C

O God, whose Son Jesus Christ is the Good Shepherd of your people: Grant that, when we hear his voice, we may know him who calls us each by name, and follow where he leads; who, with you and the Holy Spirit, lives and reigns, one God, for ever and ever. Amen.

Collect for the Fourth Sunday of Easter (2019 BCP)

BAPTISM INITIATES a lifelong journey in which Christians are invited to continually follow Jesus as Lord and consequently grow in their love and knowledge of God. The lectionary prepares people for this journey in the fourth Sunday of Easter, known as Good Shepherd Sunday, which focuses on the need for

Christians to be obedient to Jesus as sheep following a shepherd. Then, in Ordinary Time, it examines the fruit of obedience, which is the manifestation of the kingdom of God on earth. These selections from Ordinary Time use a number of agrarian symbols—seeds, soil, plants, weeds, sheep, vineyards—to describe how the kingdom of God is manifested on earth, and the ways in which the growth of the kingdom is frustrated by the continued presence of sin. This chapter will begin with an exploration of Christian obedience through the symbols of sheep and shepherd before addressing the consequences of obedience through the various agrarian parables covered by the lectionary in Ordinary Time.

Obedience: Sheep and the Shepherd

Sheep are fragile followers. As social animals, sheep stick together in flocks and follow whoever they identify as their leader. As a result, they can easily be led astray if they follow a poor or insipid leader. This potential danger is compounded by their fragility, as they are a favorite prey for a whole host of animals. For this reason, the role of the shepherd is vital, as they are responsible for keeping the flock together and guiding them to safe pastures.

Scripture routinely refers to human beings as sheep. The prophets use the term to denote the waywardness of Israel, a nation that all too easily worshiped dumb idols and ran after false gods. Such a description is also applied throughout Scripture to humanity in general. Isaiah, for instance, declares that all people, "like sheep, have gone astray, each of us has turned to our own way" (Isa. 53:6 NIV).

When human beings see references to sheep in Scripture and see sheeplike animals on farms or fields, they are invited to see themselves in these fragile and foolish followers. This can be a challenge, since we live in a world that pushes us to see ourselves as independent individuals who are reliant on no one and moved by no one. But the reality is that we are all sheep, born into an endless ocean of persuasion, with the voices of friends, family, media, and advertisements pushing and prodding us to think and act in various directions. The question is not whether we will be persuaded but who we will be persuaded by.

The readings for the fourth week of Easter use the symbols of sheep and shepherd to implore Christians to be obedient, to allow themselves to be persuaded by the teaching of Jesus above all else. In the Gospel selection for these weeks (John 10), Jesus identifies himself as the Good Shepherd and contrasts his teaching, his "voice," with the voice of the hired hand. According to Jesus, the hired hand cares only about himself and will abandon the sheep once his life is threatened (vv. 12–13). The hired hand represents all false teachers, those who attempt to persuade others to act in ways that oppose God's good and perfect will. On a deeper level, the hired hand also symbolizes all forms of human persuasion tinged by sin. Even well-intentioned efforts to persuade others often contain a modicum of selfish desire: We want others to conquer addiction so that they might no longer be a burden to us, or we want to win an argument for the thrill of being declared right.

In contrast, Jesus identifies himself as the Good Shepherd, the only one who can purely persuade since he is the only human who is without sin. Jesus has no mixed motives; he always wants what is best for us. He demonstrates the purity of his motives by dying on the cross. The Good Shepherd can thus be trusted because he lays down his life for the sheep. As Jesus states, Christians implicitly acknowledge him as the Good Shepherd by hearing his voice. They are exhorted to engage in acts of selective listening—reading and hearing the words of Scripture as the Word of God and the voice of the Shepherd and privileging these words above all others. In a word-saturated environment, a commitment to this privileged listening must be renewed each day, since each day brings with it an assault of rival voices coming from people, advertisements, and electronic devices. To combat these voices, Christians must "inwardly digest" Scripture as much as possible, reading it throughout the day, listening to it in church and on their phones, and reciting it by memory in mundane moments. In so doing, they learn to privilege the voice of the Shepherd.

But listening must be coupled with obedience to the voice of the Good Shepherd. Psalm 23 is included in the readings for the fourth week of Easter in order to exhort Christians to obey the voice of Jesus the Good Shepherd. It incorporates a number of verbs that connote obedience: The Shepherd leads, guides, and makes the sheep lie down. Verse 4 then gives the symbol of the staff, which is the preeminent symbol of obedience in Scripture. The wooden staff of Moses guided the

Israelites through the Red Sea, and this staff also healed those repentant Israelites who were snakebitten in the desert. As we saw in chapter 3, the wooden staff is also a symbol of the cross, itself a great act of obedience of the Son to the Father.

These exhortations to obey Jesus are coupled with serene depictions of love and tenderness that controvert our understandings of obedience. This culminates in the fourth verse of Psalm 23, which declares that the Shepherd's rod and staff are actually a comfort rather than a harsh burden. While subjugation and a diminishment of agency characterize many forms of human obedience, those who obey the Good Shepherd experience the comfort and freedom of a walk by still waters.

Seed, Soil, Plants: The Kingdom of God

As Christians obey the voice of Jesus the Good Shepherd, God begins to reign in their hearts, and the effects of this reign on the individual and social lives of Christians will become manifestations of the kingdom of God, physical appearances of God's will being done on earth as it is in heaven. The readings from Proper 10A, 11A, and 12A include a portion of Jesus's teachings concerning the nature, character, and growth of the kingdom of God through a number of parables. These parables are meant to capture our imaginations, giving us a picture of what life with God is supposed to look like here on earth. These parables draw from the rich symbolism of the field: seeds, soil, weeds, plants, and fruit.

Seed and soil. Seeds are the preeminent symbol of potential: A single seed carries all the genetic material necessary to produce a plant that is a thousand times its size. An acorn, for instance, contains within it everything needed to produce an enormous oak. All that is needed is for the acorn to be placed in a healthy environment, with good soil, water, and sunlight.

Throughout his kingdom parables, Jesus draws on the symbol of the seed to indicate the enormous potential of the Word of God. In the parable of the sower (Matt. 13:1–9, 18–23, Proper 10A), the seed is the Word of God, which visibly manifests the kingdom of God in the world whenever it is received by faithful hearts—those that reside in the good soil. Soil is a symbol of receptivity; it provides the necessary nutrients to promote the growth of the seed. In this parable, as well as others, soil is the symbol for the receptivity of the souls who hear the Word of God: "The diversity of ground refers to the souls of believers."[1] The seeds that are snapped up on the path are the soilless, those who do not truly hear the Shepherd's voice, while the soil full of weeds and rocks represents those whose hearts are conflicted and are thus unable or unwilling to clear out the rocks and weeds that would allow the Word to flourish in their lives. But the good soil represents those who accept the Word of God with joy and are open to the ongoing reception of Scripture (water) and God's glory (sunlight). Those in the good soil produce a large and abundant harvest, visibly manifesting God's love and beauty throughout the world.

The remainder of readings for Proper 10A show how God continues to nourish the good seed through the continual reception of his Word. The first reading of this week, Isaiah 55:10–13, states that the Word of God flows down like rain upon the earth, nurturing seeds and creating a rich harvest on the mountain. The seeds that receive this rain will receive rich spiritual nourishment that will manifest itself in joy (singing and clapping) and beauty (cypress and myrtle). The psalm for Proper 10A, Psalm 65, likewise states that God visits the earth with water and prepares the grain. God's Word is here equated with both water and seed that, when received on good soil, produce an abundance of beauty.

Weeds. Jesus tempers expectations for the visible manifestation of the kingdom of God through his inclusion of weeds in the parable of the sower. The weed is an enduring symbol of the persistence of evil in the world. Farms and gardens must constantly do battle with weeds, whose root systems are often impossible to eradicate. The seeds of some weeds can remain dormant for centuries, waiting to be activated by the churn of the plow. The green shoots of new weeds are nearly identical to neighboring plants, making it impossible for their removal not to affect healthy crops. As they grow taller, their ugliness is slowly revealed as they blot, choke, and hinder the harvest.

The parable of the sower in Proper 10A ends not with the entire earth covered in abundant crops, but rather a patchwork of healthy plants intertwined with meager saplings and weeds. These weeds are a sign that the growth of the kingdom of God cannot be completed by the church, for the presence of evil will remain until the second coming of Christ. This point is furthered by Jesus in the parable of the weeds (Matt. 13:24–30, Proper 11A): Just as the farmer's enemy sows weeds in his field to stunt the growth of his crops, so the devil continues to cultivate wicked people who frustrate the growth of the kingdom of God. Only at the final judgment will the Son of Man send his angels to sort the harvest, rooting out the wicked and hurling them into the fiery furnace.

The symbol of weeds throughout the lectionary readings reminds churches that their efforts to bring forth the kingdom of God are constantly challenged by the ubiquity of sin. Like weeds, sin cannot be eradicated by the church's efforts alone. The presence of evil, and evil persons, hinders the advancement of the kingdom and prevents its emergence from gaining wider purchase. The presence of evil persons even extends inside the church itself. Within the church there is a mixture of wheat and weeds, of good and wicked. In any given church one can encounter a group of people who all look the same—who profess the same creeds and sing the same songs—but whose hearts may or may not be aligned with their words. Just as in society there are wicked people who never break the law, within the church there are evil people whose wickedness is never revealed to the congregation. Church leaders can only discipline what they see on the outside; they cannot discipline what is hidden in the heart. The church thus continues to seek the kingdom of God, knowing that some of its members might revolt: "But in the Lord's field, which is the church, at times what was grain turns into weeds and at times what were weeds turn into grain; and no one knows what they will be tomorrow."[2]

Sprouts and trees, growth and hiddenness. Proper 10A and 11A paint a complex picture of the kingdom of God. On the one hand, those who reside in the good soil *will* produce fruit. God makes the kingdom grow as a natural outflow of obedience to his Word, and he promises that there will be a full flowering of his kingdom at the end of history. But the kind of growth manifested and the speed of this growth are not controllable by humanity. As such, the manifestation of the kingdom is often hidden from the wider world. Two parables taken from the Gospel reading of Proper 6B (Mark 4:26–34) emphasize these points. In the first parable, Jesus states, "The kingdom of God is as if someone would scatter seed on the ground, and would sleep and rise night and day, and the seed would sprout and grow, he does not know how" (vv. 26–27). The growth of the kingdom is not ultimately under the control of Christians, just as the growth of the field is not ultimately under the control of the farmer. It is God who does the growing, and those who attempt to control and manage the growth of the church will eventually find their plans frustrated.

The other parable from Proper 6B is the parable of the mustard seed. The mustard seed is known for its smallness and meagerness, but also for its extraordinary potential. Despite being the size of a pinhead, it is capable of producing a shrub large enough to be counted as a tree.

The apparent meagerness of the kingdom, like that of the mustard seed, is emphasized in the readings from Proper 12A. In the Gospel account for that day (Matt.

13:31–33, 44–52), Jesus describes the kingdom as a mustard seed, the tiniest of seeds that nevertheless becomes the greatest of shrubs. This parable is coupled with the Old Testament account of Solomon's dream (1 Kings 3:5–12), where Solomon admits that he is a meager and small child. While both the mustard seed and Solomon grow to be strong and mighty, they both begin small and insignificant. Likewise, the kingdom of God often emerges in tiny churches and in ways that are deemed insignificant to the rest of the world. The wayward soul who converts, the alcoholic who sobers up, the parents who accept a calling to foster a child, are all in themselves miraculous displays of God's kingdom breaking through. Yet such events do not seem to change the course of history. The grim headlines of the daily news, like weeds, overshadow these miracles. While there are times in which Christianity breaks forth in more spectacular ways, most of the time Christians labor knowing that their small mustard shoots will emerge as mighty trees only when Christ returns. Until that day, they can only ask for eyes to see and celebrate the small miracles that occur in their midst.

Fruits of the Kingdom: All Saints

As the parables make clear, the kingdom of God is growing even amid the wickedness of the world. While the full harvest will only be known at the end of the age, there are times in which God's kingdom brilliantly shines through, like a single Easter lily in a thicket of weeds. The church celebrates these moments during the feast of All Saints, which commemorates the lives of specific Christians who have visibly shone in extraordinary ways.

The primary text for All Saints' Day, used on years A and C, is the Beatitudes. The Beatitudes are a declaration, a pronouncement of blessedness on those of the good soil. Luke's account (6:20–31, All Saints C) emphasizes the endurance of the saints amid the weeds: The saints desire the kingdom in the midst of material poverty. They hunger and thirst for the rain of righteousness; they weep for the saplings choked by weeds. Matthew's account (5:1–12, All Saints A) emphasizes the present fruit of the harvest: The saints manifest the kingdom through peacemaking, through love and mercy, and, above all, in martyrdom. The paired readings for All Saints draw from the book of Revelation (7:9–17), Daniel (7:1–3, 15–18), and the Wisdom of Solomon (3:1–9), revealing the final flourishing of the saints, and the kingdom, on the soil of Mount Zion.

The Voice of Jesus and Obedience in the Church Today

The church continues to live out its obedience to Jesus the Good Shepherd in a number of its collective activities in Sunday worship. First and foremost, the audible recitation of Scripture in front of the entire assembly is the critical moment in which the church is called to behave like sheep, listening attentively to the Shepherd's voice. Rather than picking and choosing passages of Scripture that are agreeable to all, the oral recitation of Scripture from a predetermined lectionary provides an opportunity to hear from selections of Scripture that may be difficult or uncomfortable. This is crucial for ensuring that Christians don't admire Scripture only when it "agrees with the carnal principles which govern them."[3] But Scripture is also read out loud in order to hold the preacher accountable to the Word of God. Pastors exercise the authority of shepherds, but only if their words are in accordance with the words of the Good Shepherd. If the laity notice a discord between what is read and what is preached, they ought to question the pastor in order to determine whether such an error was accidental or due to a misunderstanding. Blatant disjunctions between Scripture and sermon might be signs of heresy, and their exposure grounds for discipline and removal of a pastor. But on a more mundane level, laity may discover that the pastor may be falling into theological drift, with sermons that barely engage with the readings just proclaimed.

The goal of the sermon is to unpack and elucidate the Scriptures read, and the voice of the pastor seeks to clarify and amplify the voice of the Good Shepherd. In reading Scripture out loud, laypeople are given the charge to keep the pastor tethered to this principal goal. Provided the pastor is keeping with this principal task, the people are in turn obliged to listen attentively to the sermon and allow themselves to be comforted and challenged by the message.

The gathering of the church represents a manifestation of the kingdom of God on earth. Glimpses of this kingdom are witnessed in the love, mercy, and peacemaking of its members. During the prayers of the people, the church is reminded of its continual struggle amid the weeds. It prays for peace amid wars, it prays for repentance amid prideful politicians, and it prays for protection for its members amid the devil's temptations. But the church also celebrates its victories, those moments when a few flowers pop up over the weeds: Flourishing mercy ministries, outreach to the lost, and youth confirmations are all acknowledged and celebrated in formal and informal announcements on Sundays. Funeral services are particularly important moments to celebrate the saintly lives of the church's members. The Anglican burial rite, for instance, commends the lives of the faithful departed as those who are "sheep of your own fold, a lamb of your own flock," while also encouraging the whole church to be inspired by their lives, to "renew our trust in your Father's love."[4]

Finally, the presence of flowers at a funeral service, as well as throughout the various life cycles of the church, are important and enduring symbols of the kingdom of God. For millennia, the church has adorned its sanctuaries and altars with various flowers symbolizing various fruits of the kingdom (lilies for purity, myrtle for love, etc.). In beholding these flowers, Christians are reminded that God will care for them as he cares for the lilies of the field. Their beauty is a sign of the hidden beauty of the kingdom, which will be fully manifested on Mount Zion.

CHAPTER 10

HEALING

Christ's Oil for Us

Epiphany 5B, Lent 5A,
Proper 13B, 18B, 21B, 1C, 5C, 6C

As you are outwardly anointed with this holy oil, so may our heavenly Father grant you the inward anointing of the Holy Spirit. Of his great mercy, may he forgive you your sins, release you from suffering, and restore you to wholeness and strength. May he deliver you from all evil, preserve you in all goodness, and bring you to everlasting life; through Jesus Christ our Lord. Amen.

Priestly Prayer of Anointing (1979 BCP)

AS CHRISTIANS are obedient to the voice of the Good Shepherd, they grow into beautiful plants that produce a variety of fruits, which are manifestations of the kingdom of God on earth. One of these fruits is healing: physical, emotional, spiritual, and psychological healing from the effects of sin on the human soul. The earthly ministry of Jesus highlights this integral connection between the kingdom of God and healing. Matthew describes the first public actions of Jesus shortly after the calling of the disciples, in which Jesus went "throughout Galilee, teaching in their synagogues and proclaiming the good news of the kingdom and curing every disease and every sickness among the people" (4:23). The lectionary readings, particularly for Ordinary Time, intersperse the teachings of Jesus with the various Gospel accounts of his healing miracles, and pair these passages with stories and prophecies of healing from the Old Testament. Through the symbols of leaves and oil, these lections highlight three aspects of healing in Holy Scripture: healing as a restoration of the senses, healing as permanent and eternal, and healing as anointing.

Healing and the Senses

Humans are sensual beings, navigating the world through sight, touch, taste, smell, and hearing. It is through these senses that we experience God's creation and cultivate relationships with others. We treat the loss of one of these senses as a deprivation of the goodness and beauty of human existence. Someone who loses their sense of taste is deprived of the joy of delicious food, and someone whose hearing fades is deprived of the blessings of the unique timbre of the voice of a loved one.

Our senses, however, are not limited to the physical realm. Human beings are also created with matching inner spiritual senses through which we navigate the world and cultivate our relationship with God. Our minds are given the capacity for inner vision, to "see" images and forms. We maintain a constant inner monologue of words that we "hear," and through which we can engage in conversations with others. We feel with our hearts and can even smell and taste in our souls: The mere remembrance of the taste of an exquisite meal can make us salivate.

It is through these spiritual senses that human beings principally interact with God. For example, in prayer we hear God's Word and we picture Jesus on the cross with our mind's eye. Our physical experience in the world is meant to train us to experience God in these ways. Augustine beautifully distills this supple connection between the senses:

> But, what do I love, when I love Thee? Not the prettiness of a body, not the gracefulness of temporal rhythm, not the brightness of light (that friend of these eyes), not the sweet melodies of songs in every style, not the fragrance of flowers and ointments and spices, not manna and honey, not limbs which can be grasped in fleshly embraces—these I do not love, when I love my God. Yet, I do love something like a light, a voice, an odor, food, an embrace, when I love my God—the light, voice, odor, food, embrace of my inner man, wherein for my soul a light shines, and place does not encompass it, where there is a sound which time does not sweep away, where there is a fragrance which the breeze does not disperse, where there is a flavor which

> eating does not diminish, and where there is a clinging which satiety does not disentwine. This is what I love, when I love my God.[1]

On Mount Eden, Adam and Eve had both their physical and inner senses attuned to God: They heard the voice of God with their physical ears and were able to taste the kingdom of God in partaking of the fruits of the various trees in the garden. However, sin led to their exile out of Eden, and with it a deterioration of both their physical and spiritual senses. All human beings likewise experience a diminishment of their physical senses at some point in their lives: "Ableness" is always a temporary condition. And even when we are in peak physical condition, all of us suffer from a deprivation of the spiritual senses. We do not hear God clearly and are often confused. Our visions of Jesus are crowded out by visions of worldly frivolities. Statements such as "the aroma of Christ" or "taste and see that the Lord is good" are hard to connect to, just as it would be difficult for someone who has never smelled to comprehend the aroma of a campfire.

Since God is the author of life and the inventor of all of the senses, an encounter with the living God through Jesus Christ holds with it the possibility of receiving sensual healing. The lectionary readings throughout the church year draw on accounts of Jesus's healing that involve both the physical and spiritual senses. The readings from Proper 18B emphasize the sensual aspect of Jesus's healing. Isaiah 35:4–7 states that the coming of the Lord will bring healing for the blind, deaf, and mute, a point echoed in the psalm's declaration that the "Lord opens the eyes of the blind" (Ps. 146:7). In the Gospel passage (Mark 7:24–37), Jesus places his fingers in the ears of a deaf man and touches his tongue, shouting "Ephphatha: be opened" (v. 34). The lections for 18B are arranged to show that the coming of Jesus is the coming of the Lord spoken of in Isaiah, and through his arrival has come a healing of the senses.

Jesus is fully human and fully divine: In him there is perfect union of the physical and the spiritual. His incarnation enables human beings to encounter God through their bodies so that they might also encounter him in their hearts. His healing ministry thus serves to repair the damage to both the physical and spiritual senses. He heals the blind so that they might see God in their mind's eye. He feeds the hungry so that they might learn to feed on him. Throughout the Gospels, Jesus uses his physical miracles as an invitation for the cured to have their inner senses healed by him. For instance, in the Gospel passage from Proper 13B (John 6:24–35), Jesus cures hunger through a miraculous multiplying of bread, and this miracle provides an invitation for the crowd to satiate their spiritual hunger through his body, which is the Bread of Life. Lent 4A features the lengthy account in John 9:1–41 of Jesus healing a man born blind, which serves as a platform for Jesus to reveal that he is the author of life and capable of healing both the outer and inner senses. The miracle begins with Jesus forming mud out of dirt and saliva, a clear reference to the forming of Adam out of dirt and breath: "He wanted to show with the mud that he himself is the one who made Adam from the earth."[2] The miracle thus discloses Jesus's identity as the Son of God who, with the Father and Spirit, is capable of healing that which he created. Jesus then invites the blind man to place his faith in the Son of God as the one capable of curing both physical and spiritual blindness.

Trees and Eternal Healing

Trees have long been associated with health, healing, and life. A healthy tree produces fruit that nourishes the body and seeds that bring about more life. A healthy tree also produces green leaves, which have been used in various medicines to bring about healing from burns, illness, and disease. Green leaves are thus a symbol of both healing and health: They are the product of a healthy tree and produce that brings about healing in others.

The Tree of Life is the preeminent mark of eternal health in Scripture. On Mount Eden, the fruit of this tree was meant to cement immortality for Adam and Eve, but this gift was denied to them by their fall into sin. Through Jesus Christ, Christians are promised access to the Tree of Life again when they are resurrected to eternal glory. According to Revelation, leaves of the Tree of Life are for the "healing of the nations" (22:2): Eternal, lasting healing will be granted to all who follow Jesus as Lord and God.

Jesus Christ stands next to the Tree of Life on the eschatological Mount Zion and grants to those who believe in him the healing fruits of this tree. According to Ephrem the Syrian, Jesus is the Divine Doctor who dispenses the products of the Tree of Life, the medicine of immortality.[3] Throughout Scripture, a return to God's presence through Jesus Christ is thus associated with healing, and the products of the Tree of Life (wood, oil from olives, and leaves) become symbols of Jesus's divine healing.

The lectionary frequently incorporates passages of Scripture that depict Jesus as a doctor, using the symbols of trees, fruit, oil, and leaves to bring about health and healing. Several Gospel passages depict Jesus performing physician-like healing. The Gospel selection for Epiphany 5B, for instance, shows Jesus performing what we might consider a routine doctor's healing, curing Simon's mother-in-law of a fever (Mark 1:29–39). Such routine healings, the kind performed with leaf-derived powders today, are often paired (as they are in this passage) with spiritual healing through the casting out of demons. The pairing of these healings shows that, as the Divine Doctor, Jesus alone is capable of bringing comprehensive healing of both body and soul.

Proper 1C focuses on the symbol of leaves, pairing a brief account of Jesus healing the diseased and demon-possessed with Old Testament arboreal imagery. Psalm 1 reveals that those whose delight is in the law of the Lord are like trees planted near streams of water, with leaves that never wither. Jeremiah 17:5–10 expands upon this image, showing how these trees are able to withstand the heat and droughts of life. Those who are planted by the streams of the water of the Holy Spirit are the ones whose leaves will remain green under persecution.[4]

But the most prominent revelation of Jesus as Divine Doctor, dispenser of the gifts of the Tree of Life, is found through his healings of those who have died. In raising individuals from the dead, Jesus shows that his healing power stretches beyond the physical and psychological, penetrating even to the place of the dead. In raising individuals from the dead, Jesus shows that he has the power to fully reverse the curse of Adam and set us on a path back to the Tree of Life. While the readings from Proper 5C show both Elijah and Jesus raising people from the dead (1 Kings 17:17–24; Luke 7:11–17), the readings from Lent 5A are meant to show how Jesus's ability to resurrect the dead reveals his ultimate and final power over the bonds of death. Ezekiel 37:1–14 shows that the pouring out of the Spirit through the breath of Jesus will bring about a revivification of dry bones that are long dead. Then, John 11:1–45 shows that Jesus can command the putrefying Lazarus to rise from the tomb through the words formed by the breath of his shout. The discourse preceding this miracle is meant to reveal to the crowd that the breath of Jesus is the same breath of God cascading through the valley in Ezekiel's vision: His discourse with Martha invites a belief in Jesus as the true source of resurrection and life.

Healing Power Given to the Church

As we have seen with the healings performed by Elijah and Elisha, the healing power of God is not restricted to Jesus but extends to all of those who have received his breath and are anointed with the oil of the Spirit. In the Old Testament, those capable of healing are limited to a select few who received a specific outpouring of the oil of the Spirit. But the sending of the Spirit in these limited cases anticipated Pentecost, where the entire people of God could now have access to the Spirit through profession in Jesus as Lord and God. As Paul notes, one of the gifts of the Spirit is the power to bring healing by the Spirit (1 Cor. 12:9, Pentecost A). The readings for Proper 21B are arranged to show how the awesome healing power of the Spirit is now made available to all who confess Christ. It begins with Numbers 11:4–6, 10–16, 24–29, in which the Spirit is poured out on seventy elders to aid Moses, who dramatically wishes that all might be given the Spirit. The Gospel reading from Mark 9:38–50 shows how the power to heal the demon-possessed has been extended even beyond the disciples to include those who heal "in the name" of Jesus. The Epistle reading from James 5:13–20 then implores the church to lay hands on the sick and anoint them with oil. We see in these readings an extension of the healing oil of the Spirit to all who confess Christ. The oil that christens Christians at their baptism is expressed from the fruit of the Tree of Life, healing sin-sick souls and energizing them to extend this healing to the world. The oil that Samuel used to anoint David is the same oil that is poured over Christians, bestowing on them their shared kingship through Christ the Anointed One. Receiving their kingly birthright, baptized Christians in turn pour out this healing power to a wounded and weary world.

Healing in the Church Today

The church continues to bring the healing of Christ into the world today through its worship, mission, and ministry. The experience of worship itself is meant to continue the process of the healing of the spiritual senses that begins at the moment of conversion. The church is the people of God on a journey to the promised land of Mount Zion, where they look forward to the complete healing of both the physical and spiritual senses. The experience of Christian worship is meant to provide a foretaste of this healing, in which all senses are healed and attuned to God. To this end, the church provides opportunities for Christians to awaken their spiritual senses by way of the five physical senses whenever they gather together for worship. The burning of incense begins to heal the spiritual sense of smell, inviting Christians to smell in their hearts the aroma of Christ, which takes away the stench of death. The recitation of Scripture out loud helps Christians distinguish between the inner voice of their souls and the inner voice of Jesus. The use of artwork and Christian imagery heals the eyes of the heart, which are constantly under threat of pollution from a barrage of false images that inundate the eyes through glowing screens and billboards. The culmination of this sensual healing comes in the reception of the Eucharist, in which the baptized are invited to see, touch, taste, and smell the bread and wine become the body and blood of Christ. The Eucharistic feast anticipates the full sensual feast waiting for Christians on top of Mount Zion, in which all physical and inner senses will be healed and attuned to Jesus Christ.

Through the continued use of holy oil, the church carries on the tradition of anointing its members to continue to extend the healing of Jesus Christ to the ends of the earth. The laying on of hands and anointing with oil at baptism marks the opening of the spiritual senses. As Cyril of Jerusalem puts it, this anointing makes converts "partakers of the good olive-tree, Jesus Christ. For [they] were cut off from the wild olive-tree, and grafted into the good one, and were made to share the fatness of the true olive-tree."[5] Similar anointings are bestowed at key points of the Christian life: Confirmation, reception into a new church, and commissioning for ministry are all moments that invite a fresh outpouring of oil to correspond with a fresh outpouring of the Holy Spirit.

Out of this outpouring of oil, the church extends the healing of Christ to a sinful and broken world. It brings the eternal healing of Christ into the world first through evangelism. In proclaiming the gospel, Christians function as divine pharmacists, dispensing the medicine of immortality by inviting the world to meet their Divine Doctor. They also extend physical, emotional, and spiritual healing through Jesus Christ in their ministry to a broken world. Sometimes such healings take the form of miracles: The blind see and the mute speak through experiences in prayer and worship. Other times, the miraculous manifests itself in smaller ways, such as when addicts break demonic habits.

All these major and minor signs of healing point to the eternal, permanent healing that will come from the leaves of the Tree of Life for those who know and trust in Jesus

Christ. The church provides assurance of this salvation to its members as they approach their physical death. In the anointing of the sick, the church pours out oil one final time on its dying members. As the oil brings a brief moment of physical health to the forehead of the dying, it reminds them of and cements in their hearts a deep-seated assurance that eternal health awaits them in their own resurrection. In this way, the anointing oil becomes in a real way the fruit of the Tree of Life, the first sign that the decay of the body is itself the beginning of eternal resurrection.

The Tree of Life on Mount Zion contains leaves that are meant "for the healing of the nations" (Rev. 22:3), and Christians receive assurance that permanent, lasting healing awaits them when they are raised into new life on this mountain. But healing is not the final end, the *telos*, of human beings. They are healed for a purpose, which is eternal communion with the resurrected Christ. Healing thus gives way to vision, an encounter with the glorified Christ face-to-face, which is anticipated in the transfiguration and ascension of Jesus Christ.

CHAPTER 11

VISION

Christ Our End

Last Epiphany A, B, C,
Ascension Day, Easter 6C

O God, who on the holy mount revealed to chosen witnesses your well-beloved Son, wonderfully transfigured, in raiment white and glistening: Mercifully grant that we, being delivered from the disquietude of this world, may by faith behold the King in his beauty; who with you, O Father, and you, O Holy Spirit, lives and reigns, one God, for ever and ever. Amen.

Collect for Transfiguration Day (1979 BCP)

THE SEASONS of Christmas and Epiphany celebrate the incarnation of Jesus and the manifestation of God's glory in and through Jesus Christ. The symbols of glory and light are used throughout these lectionary readings in order to show that Jesus truly is God with us, fully human and fully divine. Jesus comes not only to reveal the glory of God but to make a way for human beings to encounter this glory. The season of Epiphany thus culminates in the transfiguration of Jesus on Mount Tabor, the moment at which the fullness of God's glory shines in and through the human Jesus. Throughout Christmas and Epiphany, the glory of God is veiled in the flesh of Christ, inaccessible to onlookers except in brief moments of revelation, particularly in his baptism. But on Tabor, this veil is removed, and Peter, James, and John witness the fullness of God's glory in and through Jesus. But this manifestation of glory is only temporary. Soon after his death and resurrection, the resurrected Christ ascends to heaven and departs from the earth. However, the light and glory that dawned on Christmas do not fully depart with the ascending Christ, as the Holy Spirit will soon after allow this light to shine in the hearts of Christians.

On Transfiguration Sunday (the last Sunday of Epiphany), Easter 6C, and Ascension Day, the lectionary includes readings that help demarcate this in-between time of Christians. Through the transfiguration, Christians get a glimpse of their final goal, which is participation in the glory of God through a beatific vision of Christ. This vision is cemented in the Apocalypse of John (Rev. 21:10, 22–22:5, Easter 6C), which details the specific location of this vision: "a great, high mountain." Through the ascension, they are shown how a hope in this final end can be nourished through an immediate encounter with the resurrected Christ in the Spirit. The lectionary readings for the transfiguration, Easter 6C, and ascension highlight how the symbols of face, garments, and veil/cloud serve to nourish a Christian understanding of both our end and our hope in Jesus Christ.

Face

The face is the preeminent symbol of intimacy and personal relationship. It is through face-to-face conversations that acquaintances become friends. In the deepest of relationships, intimacy is spurred by prolonged gazes at each other. The transfiguration accounts from Matthew and Luke (Last Epiphany A and C) make specific mention of the radiant *face* of Christ on Tabor in order to indicate the possibility of personal encounter with God. The glory of God is not some abstract or ethereal concept, an experience of the numinous reducible to generic forms of religious experience. Instead, the glory of God shines in and through a human face and can thus be received through a personal encounter with Jesus Christ. As Gregory the Sinaite puts it, through the radiant face of Christ one receives "intimate knowledge" of the Father.[1] This is one of the primary reasons for the appearance of Moses alongside Jesus on Mount Tabor. The Exodus reading from Last Epiphany A chronicles one of the many ascents of Moses up through the clouds to the top of Sinai (Exod. 24:12–18). There, he partakes in the glory of God, yet does not, despite his pleading, see God face-to-face. Full intimacy with the Father is denied on Sinai. But Moses's appearance on Tabor differs from his visits to Sinai in two ways. First, at Jesus's transfiguration Moses gets an unclouded view of God's glory (the clouds that surround Tabor appear *after* Moses's appearance). Second, as Mark 9:2–9 and Luke 9:28–36 (Last Epiphany B and C) document, Moses is seen conversing with Jesus face-to-face. It is in this conversation that Moses has his greatest wish fulfilled: to see the Lord's face and live (Exod. 33:20).

A vision of the transfigured face of Jesus marks both the beginning and end of the Christian journey. This journey begins when we see in our hearts the glorified face of Jesus. It is through Jesus that the form of God can be made known in the human soul. We can believe in a kind of abstract deist God, who creates the world yet remains distant and removed. We can also see with our mind's eye the human Jesus, just as one might picture any other prominent historical figure. But in beholding with spiritual eyes the transfigured face of Jesus, we personally encounter the God of the universe. This point is emphasized in the lectionary through the inclusion of 2 Peter 1:16–21 in Last Epiphany A. Here, Peter gives his eyewitness account of Mount Tabor in order to punctuate his assertion that Christians do not follow "cleverly devised myths" (v. 16). The transfiguration was not a dreamlike vision of angelic beings but a flesh and blood encounter with the glory of God.

In receiving the testimony of Peter and the apostles, we are granted the possibility of an inner vision of the transfigured Christ. When we see the form of Jesus as the very form of God, the light of the Holy Spirit comes to dwell in our hearts. The inclusion of the ascent of Elijah in Last Epiphany B (2 Kings 2:1–12) draws out this connection between the glorified face and the reception of the Spirit. Before Elijah's departure, he takes Elisha with him through the waters of a parted Jordan. After giving Elisha this baptism, Elijah grants him a final wish: a double share of the Spirit. But Elijah promises this outpouring of the Spirit only if Elisha fixes his eyes on Elijah while he is ascending. The Christian journey likewise begins with a sharing in the baptism of Jesus in the River Jordan and is nourished by contemplating the transfigured face of Christ. In fixing our eyes upon Jesus, we receive a double portion of the Holy Spirit.

The eyes of the heart are opened when we see the face of the transfigured Christ, yet we yearn in the darkness of a still-sinful world for the day of Jesus's return. Then, what is seen with spiritual eyes will also be made visible to physical eyes. As Peter says, the light of the transfigured Christ is "a lamp shining in a dark place" (2 Pet. 1:19, Last Epiphany A), illuminating the human heart yet still not permeating the entirety of the spiritual and physical world. The end of the lectionary readings from Easter are meant to show how the vision of the transfigured face of Christ is meant not only to initiate the Christian journey but also to serve as its end. It is "a foretaste of the last day, when the just will shine in glory with God."[2] The last weeks of Easter for year C chronicle these last days as described in the final chapters of Revelation, which culminate in the lection for Easter 6C describing resurrected life. Here, it states that Christians will see Jesus face-to-face, and his name will be written on their foreheads (Rev. 22:4). This physical encounter with Jesus upon this mountain is the end goal of all human life. In this gaze upon the resurrected face of Christ, Christians come face-to-face with God, their spiritual eyes no longer clouded by sin and their physical eyes no longer clouded by death.

Garments

All three transfiguration accounts from the lectionary are keen to point out the change in Jesus's *garments* as they shine with the very glory of God. The brightness of these garments far surpasses what can be described by mere human language—Mark can only describe them as having a whiteness that no bleach could achieve (9:3).

Our garments are what cover us and surround us. Clothing protects us from the elements while simultaneously defining our status. Even a simple outfit can indicate someone's socioeconomic status and where they come from. Human beings are created ultimately to wear the glory of God as a kind of garment—they are meant to be *surrounded* by God's glory and *defined* by God's glory. In Eden, Adam and Eve were clothed with this glory, but their fall into sin immediately led to nakedness. While God graciously provided animal skins to cover them, these skins could only provide a modest protection from the sinful world. They were signs of God's mercy, but also a constant reminder of the garments that were lost when they fell from their Edenic glory.

When Jesus's robe was transfigured into a radiant, indescribable white, it was the first moment since the fall that a human being donned the raiment of glory. It was a sign that, through Jesus Christ, humanity might once again wear these garments. The goal of humanity is not just to see the face of Jesus, but to do so while surrounded by the glory of God, to breathe God's glory and to see through God's glory. Revelation 21:23 (Easter 6C) gives a picture of this final end, describing the atmosphere of eschatological Zion as one that has no need for the sun (see also Isa. 60:19–20). The effulgent glory of God will permeate all creation, surrounding the faithful like a robe.

But at the transfiguration, Peter mistakes Mount Tabor for Mount Zion. He longs to be immediately clothed with the radiant robes of Jesus, so he proposes the building of tents so that he can remain atop the mountain with Jesus, Moses, and Elijah. But Jesus has not come to share these garments with only Peter and the sons of Zebedee. He does not want only three men to join him on Tabor, but the nations to join him on Zion.

For this reason, the glory fades. Jesus descends Tabor and makes his way toward Jerusalem, where he will be crucified. The RCL's celebration of the transfiguration at the end of Epiphany (as opposed to on a fixed date) is meant to highlight this transition from Tabor to Golgotha. Peter cannot ascend to be clothed in glory until Jesus first descends to the dead. It is only after Jesus's death and resurrection that the first threads of humanity's heavenly robe are knit together. The lectionary readings for the ascension pick up on this symbol of clothing to indicate the share of glory that is made possible through Jesus's ascent. The selection from Ephesians for Ascension Day reveals the destination of Jesus's ascent: the right hand of the Father in the heavenly places, seated on his throne (Eph. 1:15–23). Psalm 93 describes the kingly status of Jesus seated on this throne, where he has "put on splendid apparel" (Ps. 93:1, 1979 BCP). In his ascension, Jesus becomes the first human in heaven, the first human since Adam to be clothed in the splendid raiment of the glory of the Father.

Christ ascends to make room for humanity in heaven and to empower humanity to ascend to heaven. In the Gospel reading for Ascension Day, Jesus describes this empowerment through the symbol of garments: "I am sending upon you what my Father promised; so stay here in the city until you have been *clothed* with power from on high" (Luke 24:49, emphasis added). Jesus ascends so that, together with the Father, he might send the Holy Spirit to clothe his followers with power from on high. To receive the Holy Spirit is to have our hearts surrounded by and infused with the very presence of God. The Spirit is the spiritual garment for those who believe in Christ, protecting our souls and granting us a foretaste of our final glory.

The transfiguration and ascension of Christ together make it possible for Christians, through the Holy Spirit, to see Jesus with spiritual eyes and experience a share of the glory with which he is clothed. But this vision remains inner and spiritual. Like Moses on Sinai, we cannot physically see Jesus face-to-face. Like Elisha once Elijah had ascended out of sight (2 Kings 2:12, Last Epiphany B), we tear at our earthly garments, knowing that we must still deal with the naked shame of sin. We long for a time in which we will be fully clothed, both spiritually and physically, with the glory of God. The readings for the transfiguration and ascension also chronicle these tensions and frustrations through the symbols of veil and cloud.

Veil and Cloud

From time to time throughout Scripture, God invites people to the top of mountains to see his glory. This is true for Mount Sinai, Mount Tabor (transfiguration), and the Mount of Olives (ascension). "Seeing" on these occasions refers to both the physical eyes as well as mental cognition. To see is to know, and to know is to see.

But these mountaintop moments were only temporary manifestations of God's glory, not the permanent radiance reserved for Mount Zion. Until that time, humanity's ability to see is frustrated by the continued presence of sin in the world. The lectionary readings for both the transfiguration and ascension show how the symbols of cloud and veil elucidate how this frustration is experienced.

Clouds and veils hinder sight without completely eradicating it. We can still see through a veil, and the sun can still partially illuminate through a cloud. But while they frustrate visual perception, clouds and veils often serve a protective purpose, shielding eyes and skin. Throughout Scripture, clouds and veils serve this dual purpose. In their sin, human beings cannot fully encounter God's glory and live, and so God uses both clouds and veils to enable a kind of partial experience of his glory while protecting us from the fire that would consume us. As accounts of the manifestation of God's glory, the lectionary readings from Transfiguration Sunday and Ascension Day prominently feature both clouds and veils. On Mount Tabor, Peter, James, and John cannot bear the full weight of Jesus's glorified face and are forced to shield their eyes on bended knee. A cloud then surrounds them to protect them from God's glory (Matt. 17:1–9; Mark 9:2–9; Luke 9:28–36). Likewise, the ascent of Jesus into the clouds indicates that his heavenly destination is still inaccessible to the disciples (Luke 24:50–53; Acts 1:9–11). A full, physical vision of the glorified Christ remains impossible for human beings until Jesus descends through the same clouds of his ascent.

While physical sight of the glorified Christ remains hindered, the lectionary readings for these weeks indicate that direct inner vision of Christ is now possible through the sending of the Holy Spirit. The Last Epiphany readings for year C include Exodus 34:29–35 and 2 Corinthians 3:12–4:2 to show how the present state of Christians differs from that of the Israelites. The Exodus reading concerns the veiling of Moses's face as he descended Sinai, and how this veil both prevented Israel from seeing the glory of God reflected on his face and protected them from the blinding light of this glory. Then, in 2 Corinthians, Paul shows that this veil was needed due to Israel's hardness of heart, and that it continues to cover the minds of those who reject Jesus. But through the Holy Spirit Christians have this inner veil removed; they can now see in their mind's eye a true vision of the reflected glory of God in Jesus Christ. The boldness through which Christians can encounter God here surpasses even that of Moses. On

Last Epiphany B, 2 Corinthians 4:3–6 continues to expand on this symbol of the veil: Through the Spirit, God has "shone in our hearts to give the light of the knowledge of the glory of God in the face of Jesus Christ" (v. 6). For those who refuse to believe that Jesus is the Son of God, a veil remains on their hearts.

While the Spirit grants this inner vision, the outer vision of the glorious face of Jesus Christ remains veiled. The human body is still plagued with sin and still subject to corruption, decay, and death. As such, our physical eyes are still incapable of perceiving this glory and living. While human flesh remains a kind of physical veil, the ascension of Jesus makes it possible for the human soul to ascend to heaven, to bypass these physical barriers, and to immediately access this glory in the Spirit.

This is why, in the ascension accounts, the disciples receive a blessing from Jesus and depart from the Mount of Olives with "great joy" (Luke 24:52). While they no longer see Jesus with their physical eyes, they are confident that, now clothed with the Holy Spirit, they will see his face with their inner eyes. The Christian life proceeds along this grain. On the one hand, there remain the frustrations of the veil of human flesh. We cannot physically bask in the radiance of Tabor, and we have yet to ascend to Zion. We have yet to receive our heavenly garments, and without them, our frail bodies continue to wither under the weight of sin. But while our flesh is decaying, our hearts are being renewed in the Spirit. As we cooperate with the Spirit, we encounter more and more of the beautiful face of Jesus in our mind's eye. The aches and pains of the body can become signs of hope, pointing to a day where corruptible flesh will give way to resurrected life, when what is seen with the mind's eye will merge with what is seen with the physical eye when we behold the face of our Savior on Mount Zion.

Face, Robe, and Veil in the Church Today

The ascended Jesus Christ has sent his Spirit to clothe us in glory and unveil our minds, enabling an internal vision of his transfigured and radiant face. At any moment, Christians can close their physical eyes and open their spiritual eyes to behold this face and contemplate the glory of God in and through Jesus Christ. When it comes to the spiritual senses, we are more comfortable opening the inner ear as opposed to the inner eye. Prayer in this case focuses principally on speaking to God and listening for his voice. But Jesus has opened up our spiritual eyes as well, and we are invited to simply behold his glorious face in silence, much like we would gaze silently at the face of an intimate friend.

When Christians gather for worship, they are afforded moments to contemplate the face of God. The stillness of the sanctuary before the beginning of worship invites Christians to kneel and close their eyes in contemplation of Christ. The wood of a cross and images of Jesus on canvas or stained glass serve to stimulate the spiritual eye through the rods and cones of the physical eye. Similar time is set aside after the reception of the Eucharist. Just as one might look into the face of a loved one over a quiet meal, Christians are encouraged to see the face of Jesus as they digest their heavenly meal.

The yearning to be clothed in the glory of God compels us to consider the ways in which physical dress communicates this heavenly desire. Those who are baptized are clothed in white as a sign that, through the cleansing waters, they are now clothed with glory from on high through the ascended Christ. In some traditions, pastors likewise clothe themselves in garments of white and gold just as Aaron donned robes in the tabernacle. Worship is a time to ascend the mountain and behold the glorious raiment of Christ, and the use of these garments helps to indicate the glory encountered when Christians assemble for worship.

Parishioners are also invited to dress up for church as a sign that the worship of Christ on this temporary mountain is the most important portion of their week. While what constitutes "dressing up" varies from church to church and place to place, Christians should nevertheless be mindful of how their dress might communicate their desires. Clothing oneself does not have to be a mindless, morally neutral act but can be an opportunity to worship God with beautiful attire.

The symbol of the veil is notably absent from the bulk of Christian worship, a sign that the veil that covers our minds has been removed by Jesus. When we enter the sanctuary, we have a clear vision. As we approach to receive communion, we ascend to the top of this mountain. For a moment, we are able to have both the inner and outer veil removed, to experience physically the glory of God in the reception of bread and wine. Shortly after this experience, however, the clouds that accompanied the ascended Christ return, and we must descend the mountain of the church and return to a still-sinful world. Yet we do not depart in despair but in joy. Just before departing, the pastor pronounces a blessing on the congregation that mirrors the blessing pronounced by the ascending Jesus on the disciples (Luke 24:50). Like the disciples, the congregation knows that they have been, and will continue to be, clothed with the splendid garments of the Holy Spirit. Such garments will protect them from the wickedness of sin and strengthen them to do the work of God in the world.

CONCLUSION

Melody and Harmony

> Blessed Lord, who hast caused all holy Scriptures to be written for our learning: Grant that we may in such wise hear them, read, mark, learn, and inwardly digest them, that by patience and comfort of thy holy Word, we may embrace and ever hold fast the blessed hope of everlasting life, which thou hast given us in our Saviour Jesus Christ. Amen.
>
> Collect for the Second Sunday of Advent (1662 BCP)

IN THIS BOOK I have sought to trace the connective tissue between the lectionary readings for each Sunday and to make clear their relationship to both the church year and Christian worship. My hope is that, by highlighting these connections, the book will help readers recover the early Christian approach to Scripture that presumed it to be an object of sacred time whose every word finds fulfillment in Jesus Christ. As I mentioned in chapter 1, this can be described analogously as melody and harmony. The melody of the lectionary is located in its Gospel selections, which take the church more or less in a linear way through the life, death, resurrection, and ascension of Jesus Christ. The harmony of the lectionary is found in the pairing of these Gospel selections with related texts from the Old Testament and New Testament. Preachers and hearers of the lectionary should seek to constantly glean the melody and harmony of Scripture, in the process discovering the power of Scripture to constantly vivify Christian life and worship. In order to further aid in this process, appendix C contains a list of common themes and symbols for each date of the RCL, as well as for the 1979 and 2019 BCP lectionaries. For pastors seeking a concrete example of the kind of preaching that utilizes the entirety of lectionary readings and relates those readings to worship and practice, I have included a sample sermon drawn from Lent 4B in appendix B.

While the RCL can serve as a starting point for Christians to see melody and harmony in all of Scripture, it should not be taken as the final word on the ordering of Sunday readings. Unfortunately, both the RCL and the LCM can lose their focus on these melodic and harmonic aspects of Scripture. When they include extended continuous passages drawn from a single Old Testament book or New Testament epistle, these lectionaries can replace harmony with cacophony. In addition, the seasons of Epiphany, Lent, and Easter include passages that often jump between various themes and time periods, making it harder to discern the melodic contours of Scripture. As a result, it can be difficult for clergy and laity alike to grasp the thematic strands for each church season.

Fortunately, the compilation and adaptation of lectionaries is an ongoing process. While there are some biblical readings that are essentially fixed by tradition to important days within the church year, there are plenty of Sundays where the "traditional" lectionary readings only stretch back forty or fifty years. There is still plenty of wet cement for those willing to consider modifications. In appendix A, I offer one such modification, which strives to strengthen both the melodic and harmonic contours of the lectionary. Just as this book does not claim to exhaust all the connections within the RCL, this modified lectionary does not claim to exhaust all possibilities for collating Scripture. As churches seek to recover ancient approaches to Scripture, my hope is that similar efforts of renewal will follow.

Ultimately, I hope that, as churches receive Scripture through the recitation of lections on Sunday, they will learn to receive it according to the vector established in the early church, discovering how God in his providence has arranged its persons, events, and symbols in ways that invite us to draw endless connections, plunging us deeper into the love and knowledge of himself. As Ephrem the Syrian declares, Scripture contains inexhaustible riches waiting for us to explore: "God has hidden within His words all sorts of treasures. . . . For God's word is the Tree of Life which proffers blessed fruits to you on all sides."[1] Let us each grab trowel, shovel, and sieve, embracing this treasure hunt and expecting to profit from the never-ending bounty of sacred Scripture.

APPENDIX A

A MODIFIED LECTIONARY

This modified lectionary is based on year A of the RCL. It is intended to keep traditional readings while strengthening the melodic and harmonic aspects of the lectionary. It follows a few basic principles.

Strengthen the harmony. I have eliminated all continuous readings of Scripture that are not paired to the Gospel reading. Such passages are superfluous, since most pastors are given freedom during Ordinary Time to go through single books of the Bible instead of using a lectionary. In addition, I have sought to choose passages for each Sunday that strongly correlate to the Gospel reading, often by connecting Old Testament symbols to the Gospel passage.

Strengthen the melody. I have amended the readings for Lent, Epiphany, and Easter in ways that honor their key themes and maintain their essential readings while bringing more conceptual clarity: Epiphany chronicles the beginnings of Jesus's ministry, showing how his miracles slowly reveal that he is the Son of God, culminating in the confession of Peter and the transfiguration of Jesus on the Last Sunday of Epiphany. Lent focuses on the interrelated themes of temptation, sin, forgiveness, and sacrifice, leaving the theme of baptism for Easter Vigil. Easter focuses on the chronological appearances of the resurrected Christ and links these Gospel readings with related lections.

Extend the melody. While the lectionary uses the Gospels as the principal melodic notes of Scripture, it covers the remainder of biblical history, those events before the first coming of Christ and those leading up to his second coming, in a piecemeal fashion. In order to address this issue, I have partitioned Ordinary Time into three periods: Ordinary Time AD is an eight-week period following Pentecost that details the history of the church in Acts and the last days in the book of Revelation. Acts and Revelation serve as the melodic lines in this season, with the rest of the Sunday lections chosen to pair with selections from these books. Then, a period of Ordinary Time follows the teachings and parables of Jesus, which have been the traditional focus of this season. Finally, Ordinary Time BC is an eight-week period leading up to Advent, which follows the history of God's people from Genesis through Exodus. These books serve as the melodic lines of the season, with other lections chosen to be paired with them. If churches use this lectionary starting at Ordinary Time BC and follow it through Ordinary Time AD, they will walk through the biblical narrative from Genesis through Revelation.

Date	First Reading	Psalm	Second Reading	Gospel	*Themes*
1 Advent	Zephaniah 1:7, 12–18	130	1 Thessalonians 5:1–11	Matthew 24:29–44	*Darkness and Watchfulness*
2 Advent	Isaiah 64:1–9	102:1–17	2 Peter 3:1–13	Matthew 3:1–12	*Repentance and Fire*
3 Advent	Isaiah 40:1–11	90:1–8 (9–11), 12	James 5:7–10	Matthew 11:2–11	*Preparation*
4 Advent	Isaiah 7:10–16	Canticle 15	Revelation 12:1–6	Matthew 1:18–25	*Expectation*
Christmas I	Isaiah 9:2–7	96	Titus 2:11–14	Luke 2:1–14 (15–20)	*Incarnation*
Christmas II	Isaiah 62:6–12	97	Titus 3:4–7	Luke 2:(1–7) 8–20	*Incarnation*
First Sunday After Christmas	Isaiah 52:7–10	98	Hebrews 1:1–12	John 1:1–14	*Incarnation*
Second Sunday After Christmas	Isaiah 11:1–9	84	Hebrews 2:5–18	Luke 2:41–52	*Incarnation—Jesus in the Temple*
Epiphany	Isaiah 60:1–6	72:1–7, 10–14	Ephesians 3:1–12	Matthew 2:1–12	*The Wise Men*

Date	First Reading	Psalm	Second Reading	Gospel	*Themes*
1 Epiphany	Genesis 7:17–8:14	51	1 Peter 3:8–22	Matthew 3:13–17	*Baptism of Jesus*
2 Epiphany	1 Samuel 3:1–10 (11–20)	139:1–5, 12–17	2 Peter 1:3–15	Matthew 4:18–25	*Calling of Peter*
3 Epiphany	2 Kings 5:1–19	41	James 5:13–20	Matthew 8: 1–17	*Power over Sickness*
4 Epiphany	Job 38: 1–11 (12–15), 16–18	29	Acts 16:16–18	Matthew 8:23–34	*Power over Nature and Spirits*
5 Epiphany	Jeremiah 5:18–25	146	2 Corinthians 4:1–6	John 9:1–41	*Power over Sight/ Faith*
6 Epiphany	Daniel 7:9–14	2	Colossians 2:1–15	Matthew 16:13–28	*Peter's Confession*
Last Epiphany—Transfiguration	Exodus 33:12–23	27:5–11	2 Corinthians 3:12–4:2	Matthew 17:1–9	*Transfiguration*
Ash Wednesday	Joel 2:1–2, 12–17 or Isaiah 58:1–12	103:8–18	2 Corinthians 5:20b–6:10	Matthew 6:1–6, 16–21	*Repentance and Fasting*
1 Lent	Genesis 2:15–17; 3:1–7	91	Romans 5:12–19	Matthew 4:1–11	*Temptation and Fasting*

Date	First Reading	Psalm	Second Reading	Gospel	Themes
2 Lent	Numbers 21:4–9	140	1 Corinthians 10:1–13	John 3:14–21	*Temptation Conquered Through Christ*
3 Lent	Genesis 33:1–16	32	1 John 1:5–10	Luke 15:1–3, 11b–32	*Repentance and Forgiveness*
4 Lent	Genesis 22:1–14	66:12–18	Hebrews 11:8–19	John 12:20–33	*The Need for Sacrifice*
5 Lent	Isaiah 1:1–20	51:7–19	Hebrews 9:11–22	John 2:13–22	*Sacrifice Only Through Christ*
Palm Sunday	Zechariah 9:9–12	118:19–29	Revelation 5:8–14	Matthew 21:1–11	*Worship*
Maundy Thursday	Exodus 12:1–4 (5–10), 11–14	116:1–2, 12–19	1 Corinthians 11:23–26	John 13:1–17, 31b–35	*Communion/New Commandment*
Good Friday	Isaiah 52:13–53:12	22	Hebrews 10:16–25	John 18:1–19:42	*The Cross*
Holy Saturday	Jonah 2:1–10	31:1–4, 15–16	1 Peter 4:1–8	John 19:38–42	*Burial and Descent to the Dead*
Easter Sunday	Acts 10:34–43	118:1–2, 14–24	Colossians 3:1–11	Matthew 28:1–10	*Resurrection*

Date	First Reading	Psalm	Second Reading	Gospel	*Themes*
2 Easter	Genesis 17:1–8 (9–14), 15–16	112	Romans 4:13–25	John 20:19–31	*Faith in the Resurrection*
3 Easter	Ezekiel 37:1–14	30	1 Corinthians 15:35–49	Luke 24:36–49	*Resurrection Is Flesh and Blood*
4 Easter	Exodus 16:11–15 (16–20), 21–35	34:8–14	Ephesians 4:1–16	Luke 24:13–35	*The Road to Emmaus*
5 Easter	Genesis 14:14–20	36:5–12	1 Corinthians 10:14–22	John 21:1–14	*Breakfast on the Beach*
6 Easter	Genesis 28:10–22	113	Acts 1:1–5	John 14:1–7, 25–31	*Preparation of Ascension and Pentecost*
Ascension	2 Kings 2:1–12	47	Philippians 2:1–12	Luke 24:44–53	*Ascension*
Pentecost	Genesis 11:1–9	104:25–35, 37	Acts 2:1–21	John 15:26–27; 16:4b–15	*Pentecost*
Trinity Sunday	Proverbs 8:1–4, 22–31	8 or Canticle 13	Romans 8:12–17	John 16:1–15	*Trinity Sunday*
Ordinary Time—AD	Acts 6:8–15; 7:44–60; 8:1	96	Philippians 1:12–26	Matthew 28:16–20	*Mission—Proclamation*

Date	First Reading	Psalm	Second Reading	Gospel	*Themes*
Ordinary Time—AD	Acts 9:1–19	67	Galatians 3:15–29	John 10:1–18	*Mission—Gathering*
Ordinary Time—AD	Acts 2:37–47	122	1 Peter 2:1–12	John 17:6–19	*The Church*
Ordinary Time—AD	Numbers 11:24–30	133	1 Corinthians 12:3b–13	John 17:20–26	*Spirit Given to All for the Church*
Ordinary Time—AD	Revelation 20:7–20	59	2 Thessalonians 1:5–12	Matthew 22:1–14	*Revelation—Judgment*
Ordinary Time—AD	Daniel 12:1–4	16	1 Thessalonians 4:13–18	John 11:1–45	*Resurrection*
Ordinary Time—AD	Revelation 21:9–27	87	Hebrews 12	Matthew 22:1–14	*Revelation—Mount Zion*
Ordinary Time—AD	Revelation 22:1–7	45	Song of Songs 2:8–17	John 2:1–12	*Revelation—Face and Wedding*
Ordinary Time—Holy Teaching	Deuteronomy 5:1–22	119:1–8	2 John 4–11	Matthew 5:1–12	*Sermon on the Mount—Beatitudes*
Ordinary Time—Holy Teaching	Leviticus 19:1–18	1	Galatians 5:13–26	Matthew 5:13–20	*Sermon on the Mount—The Law*

Date	First Reading	Psalm	Second Reading	Gospel	*Themes*
Ordinary Time—Holy Teaching	Genesis 4:1–16	37:1–18	1 John 3:7–24	Matthew 5:21–26, 38–48	*Sermon on the Mount—Hatred and Murder*
Ordinary Time—Holy Teaching	Micah 2:10–16	119:9–16	1 Corinthians 6:12–20	Matthew 5:27–32	*Sermon on the Mount—Adultery and Divorce*
Ordinary Time—Holy Teaching	Leviticus 22:17–33	37:19–28	Acts 5:1–11	Matthew 6:1–4, 19–24	*Sermon on the Mount—Money*
Ordinary Time—Holy Teaching	Isaiah 5:1–7	126	James 1:1–18	Matthew 13:1–23	*Parable of the Sower*
Ordinary Time—Holy Teaching	Hosea 10:1–8	107:33–43	Jude 5–23	Matthew 13:24–30, 36–43	*Parable of the Weeds*
Ordinary Time—Holy Teaching	Ezekiel 17:22–24	92:1–4 (5–11), 12–15	1 Corinthians 1:18–31	Matthew 13:31–35	*Parable of the Mustard Seed and Leaves*

Date	First Reading	Psalm	Second Reading	Gospel	*Themes*
Ordinary Time—Holy Teaching	Proverbs 2:1–11	119:97–104	2 Corinthians 4:1–12	Matthew 13:44–52	*Parables of Treasure*
Ordinary Time—BC	Genesis 1	104:1–25	Hebrews 4:1–11	John 1	*Creation*
Ordinary Time—BC	Genesis 2:4–25	139:1–17	Colossians 1:15–20	John 7:37–39	*Adam and Eve*
Ordinary Time—BC	Genesis 3	51	Romans 5:12–17	John 19:31–37	*The Fall*
Ordinary Time—BC	Genesis 12:1–8	105:1–15	Romans 4:1–17	John 8:42–59	*Calling of Abraham*
Ordinary Time—BC	Exodus 12:1–13	116	1 Corinthians 11:23–26	Matthew 26:17–30	*Passover*
Ordinary Time—BC	Exodus 14:10–25	Miriam's Song	1 Corinthians 10:1–13	John 3:1–17	*Crossing the Red Sea*
Ordinary Time—BC	Exodus 19:1–22	24	Hebrews 8:1–13	Matthew 24:15–31	*The Mountain and the Cloud*
Ordinary Time—BC	Exodus 40: (1–16) 17–38	66:8–20	Hebrews 9:1–14	John 2:13–22	*Tabernacle/Temple*

APPENDIX B

A SAMPLE SERMON

Below is a sample sermon, adapted from a homily given at a small church gathering in a nursing home. My hope is that this sermon exemplifies the type of message that can be given using all four of the Sunday lectionary readings, as well as showing how the approach to Scripture outlined in this book can be appropriated within nonacademic environments.

Snakes and Staves

Lent 4B

Numbers 21:4–9

Ephesians 2:1–10

John 3:14–21

Psalm 107:1–3, 17–22

One of my favorite activities when I lived in Pennsylvania was hiking along the various mountain trails that surrounded my hometown. Often during these hikes my mind would drift in all sorts of directions, and I would find myself lost in the wilderness. On one of these hikes, my mind began to wander as usual, when suddenly I noticed a rattlesnake slithering just a few feet ahead of me. Luckily, I snapped out of my mental daze and turned around and headed down a different path.

I'm sure some of you have had similar encounters with snakes, or perhaps you know someone who has even been bitten by a snake. If so, you know how suddenly snakes can show up, and how deadly they can be for those who aren't paying attention to where they are going. Venomous snakes strike fear in us, and they should. There is nothing you can do to save yourself once you have been bitten by a rattlesnake—someone else has to save you, someone else has to give you the antivenom.

In the Bible, snakes are symbols of Satan, of temptation, and of sin. We see this in the very beginning of the Bible, where Satan inhabited a snake in the garden of Eden, tempting Eve to commit the first sin. Throughout the Bible, temptation comes in the form of a snake, and when someone succumbs to sin, it is symbolized by a bite from a venomous snake.

We see this most clearly in our Old Testament reading today. In this passage, the Israelites are wandering in the desert, and they begin to complain. They are tired and they have not had enough food or drink. And they don't like the food that they do have. In hindsight, this grumbling seems ridiculous to us. After all, the Israelites have witnessed God miraculously rescue them from slavery by sending plagues on the Egyptians. They saw God part the Red Sea so that they could escape Egypt. He provided them food—manna—to eat on their journey to the promised land. And yet, even despite all these incredible things, they complain about not having good enough food to eat! They would rather be slaves and eat stew than be free and eat bread. As a result of their complaining, venomous serpents emerge out of the woods and bite and kill many of the Israelites. Their discomfort led them to succumb to temptation and sin. As Paul states in our passage from Ephesians, they followed their fleshly passions, their desires to fill their stomachs, and as a result wound up following the ruler of the power of the air. And their sinful complaining led to their death.

We might be stunned at the disobedience and whininess of the Israelites. How could they complain when God had done so much for them? But when we step back and think about our own lives, we should find that we are really not that different from the Israelites in the wilderness. We have been set free of our slavery to sin through the blood of Jesus Christ, we have been led by the Spirit through the waters of the Red Sea in our baptism, and we too are on our way to the promised land of Mount Zion. Yet, despite Jesus saving us from death and promising us eternal life, we still grumble quite a lot. Satan tempts us to be discontented with our lives. He conjures up images of our past life in Egypt, before we knew Jesus. He wants us to think of all the things we gave up by following Jesus, and he wants us to disobey God by coveting these things. When we indulge these desires, we ingest some of Satan's venom.

We become less thankful and more bitter. We compare our material blessings to those who have more than us. We lose sight of our final goal, which is to meet Jesus in the promised land.

What can we do when we find ourselves tempted and snakebitten? Our readings today invite us to *remember* when we are tempted and *look to the cross* when we are snakebitten. First, we are called to remember. Just as I was almost bitten by a rattlesnake because I forgot where I was going, Israel succumbed to temptation because they forgot all that God had done for them. Their memories of freedom were overtaken by their remembrances of a hearty meal, and this led them to sin. In order that we don't succumb to the same fate, we ought to remember all the mighty works of God, what he has done for us and all of his people. Fortunately, God constantly exhorts us to give thanks through the Psalms. The Psalms are peppered with joyous remembrances and invocations to give thanks. The first three verses of our psalm today are a great example of this: "Give thanks to the Lord, for he is good, and his mercy endures for ever. Let all those whom the Lord has redeemed proclaim that he redeemed them from the hand of the foe. He gathered them out of the lands; from the east and from the west, from the north and from the south" (107:1–3, 1979 BCP).

We remember in order to protect us from temptation. But what happens when we succumb and are snakebitten? God gave the Israelites a cure for the venom. Moses placed a bronze serpent on a wooden pole, and when the people looked at the bronze and wood, they were healed. In raising their sights high to the wooden staff, they remembered that God conquered the serpent Pharoah, and they had faith that God could also heal the deadly effects of the serpent's bite. The act of looking up was an act of faith and trust that the most merciful God could bring about forgiveness for their disobedience and heal the effects of their sin.

In our Gospel passage today, Jesus says that "just as Moses lifted up the serpent in the wilderness, so must the Son of Man be lifted up, that whoever believes in him may have eternal life" (John 3:14–15). Jesus was lifted high on the cross to conquer the serpent Satan. Those who lift their eyes high to the cross and believe in him have confidence that the venomous bite of Satan will not lead to their eternal death. Instead, he will heal the hearts of the faithful and bring them to eternal life. When we lift our heads high to see this wooden cross at church, we are invited to renew our faith in the only one who can conquer the serpent and its bite. When we look to the cross, we remember Christ's death for us, we are invited to confess our sins and receive healing from the venom we've ingested, and we can trust that the wood of this cross will lead us all the way to our promised land of Mount Zion.

In just a few moments, we will be invited to remember all the great and mighty works of God by professing our faith in the words of the Nicene Creed. As you recite these words, I invite you to let the memory of the life, death, and resurrection of Jesus rise to the front of your minds. Throughout the week ahead, let this memory protect you from the temptations to complain and disobey. At the end of our service, this wooden cross will be taken out of the sanctuary. As you follow close behind, lift your eyes up to it, and continue to rely on the mercy of Jesus throughout your week. As you find yourself tempted in the wilderness of life, look to it and know how much Jesus has done for you. When you fall into sin and become subject to evil and death, look up and know that God's mercy continues to be poured out upon you. And just as the wooden staff of Moses led the Israelites through the wilderness, the wood of this cross will lead you through your present discomforts and set you firmly in your eternal promised land.

APPENDIX C

INDEX *of* THEMES *for the* RCL *and* BCP LECTIONARIES

	RCL, 1979 BCP, 2019 BCP
Advent 1A	Judgment
Advent 1B	Judgment
Advent 1C	Judgment
Advent 2A	Repentance
Advent 2B	Judgment
Advent 2C	Repentance, Fire
Advent 3A	Glory
Advent 3B	Baptism, Redemption
Advent 3C	Repentance
Advent 4A	Joseph, Salvation
Advent 4B	Mary, Zion
Advent 4C	Mary
Christmas I	Glory and Light
Christmas II	Salvation, Redemption

	RCL, 1979 BCP, 2019 BCP
Christmas III	Glory and Light
1st Christmas	Glory and Light
2nd Christmas	Salvation, Exodus
Epiphany	Glory and Gold
Epiphany 1A	Baptism
Epiphany 1B	Baptism
Epiphany 1C	Baptism
Epiphany 2A	Calling
Epiphany 2B	Calling
Epiphany 2C	Heavenly Feast, Wine
Epiphany 3A	Calling, Redemption
Epiphany 3B	Calling, Proclamation
Epiphany 3C	Scripture, Fulfillment
Epiphany 4A	Beatitudes
Epiphany 4B	Healing
Epiphany 4C	Scripture, Fulfillment
Epiphany 5A	Scripture, Fulfillment
Epiphany 5B	Healing
Epiphany 5C	Calling
Ash Wednesday	Fasting, Repentance
Lent 1A	Temptation
Lent 1B	Baptism
Lent 1C	Temptation
Lent 2A	Faith
Lent 2B	Faith
Lent 2C	Faith
Lent 3A	Baptism, Water
Lent 3B	Decalogue, Temple
Lent 3C	Repentance
Lent 4A	Blindness, Faith
Lent 4B	Temptation

	RCL, 1979 BCP, 2019 BCP
Lent 4C	Repentance, Forgiveness
Lent 5A	Healing
Lent 5B	Crucifixion, Death
Lent 5C	Oil, Restoration
Palm Sunday	Sacrifice, Worship
Spy Wednesday	Betrayal
Maundy Thursday	Communion, Love
Good Friday	Sacrifice
Holy Saturday	Death
Easter	Resurrection
Easter 2A	Faith, Mission
Easter 2B	Faith
Easter 2C	Faith
Easter 3A	Communion, Resurrection
Easter 3B	Resurrection
Easter 3C	Eternal Life, Resurrection, Communion
Easter 4A	Communion, Church
Easter 4B	Obedience, Shepherd
Easter 4C	Eternal Life, Resurrection
Easter 5A	Mission, Church
Easter 5B	Obedience, Judgment
Easter 5C	Eternal Life, Resurrection, Mission
Easter 6A	Holy Spirit, Obedience
Easter 6B	Commandments, Obedience
Easter 6C	Eternal Life, Resurrection
Easter 7A	Glory, Ascension
Easter 7B	Mission, Church
Easter 7C	Mission
Ascension	Ascension, Mission
Pentecost	Holy Spirit, Mission
Trinity Sunday	Trinity

	RCL, 1979 BCP, 2019 BCP
Proper 1A	Commandments, Murder, Adultery
Proper 1B	Healing
Proper 1C	Healing
Proper 2A	Commandments, Forgiveness
Proper 2B	Healing
Proper 2C	Forgiveness, Reconciliation
Proper 3A	Possessions, Anxiety
Proper 3B	Fasting, Wedding
Proper 3C	Speech, Deed and Word
Proper 4A	Commandments, the Word
Proper 4B	Healing, Sabbath
Proper 4C	Healing, Gentiles
Proper 5A	Healing, Forgiveness
Proper 5B	Satan, Serpent
Proper 5C	Healing
Proper 6A	Obedience, Mission
Proper 6B	The Kingdom of God
Proper 6C	Healing
Proper 7A	Rejection, Discipleship
Proper 7B	Wind, Water
Proper 7C	Healing, Swine, Demons
Proper 8A	Prophets, the Poor
Proper 8B	Healing
Proper 8C	Discipleship
Proper 9A	Rejection, Discipleship
Proper 9B	Wisdom, Mission
Proper 9C	Mission
Proper 10A	The Kingdom of God
Proper 10B	Judgment, John the Baptist
Proper 10C	Commandments, Love
Proper 11A	The Kingdom of God

	RCL, 1979 BCP, 2019 BCP
Proper 11B	Healing, Shepherd
Proper 11C	Sabbath, Rest
Proper 12A	The Kingdom of God
Proper 12B	Communion
Proper 12C	Prayer, Supplication
Proper 13A	Bread, Feast
Proper 13B	Healing, Communion
Proper 13C	Greed, Possessions
Proper 14A	Faith, Protection
Proper 14B	Bread, Life
Proper 14C	Watchfulness
Proper 15A	Holiness, Healing
Proper 15B	Bread, Wine, Communion
Proper 15C	Judgment, Separation
Proper 16A	Salvation, Temptation
Proper 16B	Blood, Communion
Proper 16C	Sabbath, Healing
Proper 17A	Discipleship
Proper 17B	Works, Hypocrisy
Proper 17C	The Poor, Feasting
Proper 18A	Forgiveness, Reconciliation
Proper 18B	Healing
Proper 18C	Obedience, Discipleship
Proper 19A	Forgiveness
Proper 19B	Crucifixion, Discipleship
Proper 19C	Mercy, the Lost
Proper 20A	Forgiveness, Mercy
Proper 20B	Crucifixion, Humility
Proper 20C	The Kingdom of God
Proper 21A	Forgiveness, Mercy
Proper 21B	Healing

	RCL, 1979 BCP, 2019 BCP
Proper 21C	The Kingdom of God, Judgment
Proper 22A	Commandments, Judgment
Proper 22B	Marriage, Divorce
Proper 22C	The Kingdom of God
Proper 23A	Judgment, Wedding Feast
Proper 23B	Wealth, Possessions
Proper 23C	Healing, Worship
Proper 24A	Rulers, Authority
Proper 24B	Discipleship, Ransom
Proper 24C	Prayer, Struggle
Proper 25A	Judgment, Authority
Proper 25B	Faith, Blindness, Healing
Proper 25C	Humility
Proper 26A	Hypocrisy, Humility
Proper 26B	Commandments, Love
Proper 26C	Repentance, Salvation
Proper 27A	Wedding Feast, Judgment
Proper 27B	Widows, Provision
Proper 27C	Marriage, Resurrection
Proper 28A	Judgment
Proper 28B	Judgment
Proper 28C	Judgment
Proper 29A	Judgment
Proper 29B	Throne, Judgment
Proper 29C	Judgment, Separation
All Saints	The Kingdom of God

NOTES

Introduction

1. Ephraim Radner, "The Intersection Between Our Lives and Biblical History," *Credo*, February 12, 2024, https://credomag.com/2024/02/the-intersection-between-our-lives-and-biblical-history/.

2. Thomas K. Carroll, *Preaching the Word* (Michael Glazier, 1984), 16.

3. J. Scott Duvall and J. Daniel Hays, *Grasping God's Word: A Hands-On Approach to Reading, Interpreting, and Applying the Bible*, 4th ed. (Zondervan, 2020).

4. Gordon D. Fee and Douglas K. Stuart, *How to Read the Bible for All Its Worth*, 4th ed. (Zondervan, 2014), 77.

5. N. T. Wright, *The New Testament and the People of God* (Fortress, 1996).

6. Michael Legaspi argues that the rise of the historical-critical method explicitly sought to render the Old Testament as dead history. He says that one of its founders, Johann Michaelis, argued for "an explicit recognition of the Old Testament's deadness, its status as an ancient literary corpus discontinuous both with Christianity and with Judaism." Michael C. Legaspi, *The Death of Scripture and the Rise of Biblical Studies* (Oxford University Press, 2011), 6.

Chapter 1 Judgment

1. Augustine, *City of God*, 19.21.

2. "The Lighting of the Paschal Candle," *The Book of Common Prayer* (Church Publishing, 1979), 286.

3. Ignatius of Loyola, *Spiritual Exercises*, paragraph 65.

4. Maximus the Confessor, *On the Ecclesiastical Mystagogy*, trans. Jonathan J. Armstrong (St Vladimir's Seminary Press, 2019), 77.

Chapter 2 Glory

1. Justin Martyr, *The First Apology, The Second Apology, Dialogue with Trypho, Exhortation to the Greeks, Discourse to the Greeks, The Monarchy of the Rule of God*, trans. Thomas B. Falls, The Fathers of the Church 6 (Catholic University of America Press, 1948), 107.

Chapter 3 Repentance

1. Ephrem the Syrian, *Songs for the Fast and Pascha*, trans. Blake Hartung, Joshua Falconer, and J. Edward Walters, The Fathers of the Church 145 (Catholic University of America Press, 2022), 52.

Chapter 4 Sacrifice

1. Augustine, "Tractate 120 on the Gospel of John," quoted in *John 11–21*, ed. Joel C. Elowsky, vol. 4b of *Ancient Christian Commentary on Scripture, New Testament*, ed. Thomas C. Oden (InterVarsity, 2007), 328.

2. Augustine of Hippo, "Lectures or Tractates on the Gospel According to St. John," in *St. Augustine: Homilies on the Gospel of John, Homilies on the First Epistle of John, Soliloquies*, ed. Philip Schaff, trans. John Gibb and James Innes, vol. 7, *A Select Library of the Nicene and Post-Nicene Fathers of the Christian Church, First Series* (Christian Literature Company, 1888), 299.

3. Those liturgies that hold this declaration in the present tense only (Christ *is* sacrificed for us) best draw out this reality.

4. Heinrich Salmuth, "Seventh Sermon on the Passion," in *Luke*, ed. Beth Kreitzer, vol. 3, *Reformation Commentary on Scripture, New Testament III*, ed. Timothy George and Schott M. Manetsch (IVP Academic, 2015), 470.

Chapter 5 Resurrection

1. Romano Guardini, *The Lord* (Gateway Editions, 2012), 583.

2. Michael Niebauer, *Four Mountains: Encountering God in the Bible from Eden to Zion* (Lexham Press, 2025), 41–43.

3. In light of this passage and the feasts of the multiplication of fish and loaves, fish have been associated with the wine consumed during

the communion meal. Like the animals used in temple sacrifices, fish have blood that is expelled as they are prepared for consumption. In addition, the symbol of the fish soon became associated with Jesus Christ, with the Greek word for "fish," *ichthys*, being used as an acrostic for his life and work. According to Augustine, Jesus is the "great fish" who was the first to come up out of the sea. Saint Augustine, *Homilies on the Gospel of John 1–40*, ed. Allan D. Fitzgerald, trans. Edmund Hill, vol. 12, *The Works of Saint Augustine: A Translation for the 21st Century*, ed. Boniface Ramsey (New City Press, 2009), 315.

Chapter 6 Wind and Fire

1. *Didascalia Apostolorum*, trans. Hugh Connolly (1929), vi.22.
2. "Alternative Forms of the Great Thanksgiving," *The Book of Common Prayer* (Church Publishing, 1979), 369.
3. Athanasius and Didymus, *Works on the Spirit: Athanasius's Letters to Serapion on the Holy Spirit and Didymus's On the Holy Spirit*, trans. Mark DelCogliano, Andrew Radde-Gallwitz, and Lewis Ayres, Popular Patristics Series 43 (St Vladimir's Seminary Press, 2011), 160.

Chapter 7 Communion

1. Michael Niebauer, *Virtuous Persuasion: A Theology of Christian Mission* (Lexham Press, 2022), 233.
2. Nicholas Afanasiev, *The Church of the Holy Spirit*, ed. Michael Plekon, trans. Vitaly Permiakov (University of Notre Dame Press, 2007), 34.

Chapter 8 Faith

1. Cyril of Jerusalem, *Lectures on the Christian Sacraments: The Procatechesis and the Five Mystagogical Catecheses*, ed. F. L. Cross, Popular Patristics Series 2 (St Vladimir's Seminary Press, 1977), 64.
2. Cyril of Jerusalem, *Lectures*, 60.

Chapter 9 Obedience

1. Jerome, *Commentary on Matthew*, trans. Thomas P. Scheck, The Fathers of the Church 117 (Catholic University of America Press, 2008), 155.
2. Augustine, "Sermon 73A.1," quoted in *Matthew 1–13*, ed. Manlio Simonetti, vol. 1, *Ancient Christian Commentary on Scripture, New Testament*, ed. Thomas C. Oden (InterVarsity, 2001), 277.

3. John Henry Newman, "Knowledge of God's Will without Obedience," in *John Henry Newman: Selected Sermons*, ed. Ian Ker, The Classics of Western Spirituality, ed. Bernard McGinn (Paulist Press, 1994), 71.

4. "The Burial of the Dead: Rite Two," *The Book of Common Prayer* (Church Publishing, 1979), 498–99.

Chapter 10 Healing

1. Augustine of Hippo, *Confessions*, trans. Vernon J. Bourke, The Fathers of the Church 21 (Catholic University of America Press, 1953), 269–70.

2. Amonius, in *John 1–10*, ed. Joel C. Elowsky, vol. 4a, *Ancient Christian Commentary on Scripture, New Testament*, ed. Thomas C. Oden (InterVarsity, 2006), 324.

3. Ephrem the Syrian, *Ephrem the Syrian: Hymns*, trans. Kathleen E. McVey, The Classics of Western Spirituality (Paulist Press, 1989), 276.

4. "It goes on to say that he will not fear when the heat comes, meaning either a time of persecution or the day of judgment, and that his leaf will remain green (or that his branches will remain leafy), such that he should never fear aridity, for the grace of all the virtues will germinate." Jerome, in *Jeremiah, Lamentations*, ed. Dean O. Wenthe, vol. 12, *Ancient Christian Commentary on Scripture, Old Testament*, ed. Thomas C. Oden (InterVarsity, 2009), 134.

5. Cyril of Jerusalem, *Lectures*, 60.

Chapter 11 Vision

1. Gregory the Sinaite, "Discourse on the Holy Transfiguration," in *Light on the Mountain: Greek Patristic and Byzantine Homilies on the Transfiguration of the Lord*, trans. Brian E. Daley, Popular Patristics Series 48 (St Vladimir's Seminary Press, 2013), 348.

2. Philagathos, "On the Saving Transfiguration," in *Light on the Mountain: Greek Patristic and Byzantine Homilies on the Transfiguration of the Lord,* trans. Brian E. Daley, Popular Patristics Series 48 (St Vladimir's Seminary Press, 2013), 264.

Conclusion

1. Ephrem the Syrian, *Commentary on the Diatessaron*, quoted in *Treasure-House of Mysteries: Explorations of the Sacred Text through Poetry in the Syriac Tradition*, trans. Sebastian Brock, Popular Patristics Series 45 (St Vladimir's Seminary Press, 2012), 28.

MICHAEL NIEBAUER is director of Heritage Mission, an initiative that trains leaders to start worship services in care facilities. He is the author of *Four Mountains: Encountering God in the Bible from Eden to Zion* and the award-winning *Virtuous Persuasion: A Theology of Christian Mission.*

CONNECT WITH MICHAEL

MichaelNiebauer.com

@MikeNiebauer

@RevNiebauer